MW00712511

"The Creator empowered you to overcome obstacles rather than merely endure and survive this life. It's called *Resilience*. In this crucial hour, it's vital that you identify and realize this power for yourself and bring those around you to a place of victory. I believe our dear friend, Colleen Rouse, has crafted a beautiful message that will draw this virtue out of you."

—JOHN BEVERE, author and Minister at Messenger International

"Trials are the proving ground for every leader. They have the power to reveal hidden strengths. In *Resilience*, Colleen helps us identify and hone these latent strengths so you can emerge victorious in struggles large and small."

—LISA BEVERE, *New York Times* bestselling author

"Thank you for all you do for the benefit of those around you. Never forget how valuable you are. Run your race well!"

—BILLY HUMPHREY, founder of
International House of Prayer, Atlanta

"Books like babies are born when an author and a message collide. My good friend Colleen Rouse's book *Resilience* emanates from her being—who she is. I have known Colleen Rouse for almost three decades and know that this book doesn't merely contain information and inspiration rather, it will draw out of you your own resiliency that might be dormant and needs a voice to awaken it. You will love this book and get one for all those you love."

—SAM CHAND, leadership consultant
and author of *Leadership Pain*

Published by Thrive Today

For foreign and subsidiary rights, contact the author.

Cover design by: Sara Young

ISBN: 978-1-954089-33-4   1 2 3 4 5 6 7 8 9 10

Printed in the United States of America

RESILIENCE

IT'S TIME TO GET UP

THR!VE T*DAY

FOREWORD

What a privilege it is to have this opportunity to write the foreword for my amazing wife of 38 years and her new book, *Resilience*! When I think about the actual definition of resilience, able to withstand or recover quickly from difficult conditions, I realize that if we've ever needed a book about this subject, this is the time! Never in my life have I witnessed so many people struggling with life as everyone is trying to recover from all the challenges we faced in 2020. With the pandemic, racial tension, economic challenges, and national division, each day has been a challenge to keep moving forward when everything seems to be falling apart.

Over the years, I've watched countless people who just don't handle difficulty well. All it takes is for something negative to go wrong, and they're down for the count and are never the same again. Think about how many people you know who can trace back their inner turmoil to one event that rocked their world and they just never fully recovered enough to completely let go and move forward.

That's why if you're going to bounce back and rise to the life to which God has called you,, you're going to need the power of resilience to make it. I really believe it is the separating factor in most people's lives. My wife, Colleen has modeled this concept of resilience since I met her almost 40 years ago. From going through serious physical challenges in her early life, to losing friends and family because of her Christian faith, to experiencing all the emotional ups and downs of pastoring thousands of people over the last 31 years, her ability to withstand and recover quickly has been at the very core of her success in life.

I'm so excited you're reading this book! You're about to experience some of the most amazing stories and principles that have the potential to take you into a life you may have never imagined. So get ready for a life of overcoming obstacles and achieving everything God has put you on this earth for!

—Dennis Rouse

CONTENTS

Introduction 9

Chapter 1. AIN'T I A WOMAN:
Resiliency is Inherent. 15

Chapter 2. FOR THE GOOD:
Resiliency Renews Perspective 23

Chapter 3. THE SPACE BETWEEN:
Resiliency Reshapes Suffering 33

Chapter 4. THE ONE LESS TRAVELED:
Resiliency is Pathway. 41

Chapter 5. WHEN WE SAY YES:
Resiliency is Ignited by Obedience 51

Chapter 6. CALM IN THE STORM:
Resilience Cultivates Composure. 63

Chapter 7. NO MORE OFFENSE:
Resiliency is Linked to Humility. 71

Chapter 8. FIERCE AND FOCUSED:
Resiliency Creates Stability and Tenacity. 79

Chapter 9. THE INERTIA OF EMPATHY:
Resilience is a Catalyst for Compassion 89

EPILOGUE: Love of God is The Core of Resilience 101

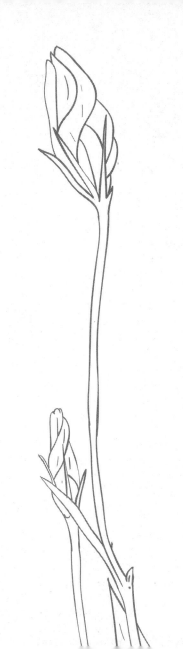

❧ INTRODUCTION ❧

When professional stunt woman Jessie Graff completed the American Ninja Warrior course in 2016 with twelve seconds on the clock, she was the first woman in history to do so. When asked what she hoped people would take away from her remarkable run, she responded, "You're stronger than you think. You can conquer almost any obstacle, if you're willing to work for it."

In subsequent interviews, she went on to say, "Expect things to feel impossible at first, but do the progressions, and your perception of impossible will change."

If you're anything like me, chances are you are not planning to participate in American Ninja Warrior anytime soon. However, I do hope you are planning to participate in life. Believe it or not, there are multiple parallels between America Ninja Warrior and this thing we call life. Perhaps of greatest note, every obstacle along that course is designed to take the competitor out.

While life isn't specifically designed with adverse intent, I think we can all agree that our daily routines are a crash course in survival, especially of late. The pandemic has tested every one of us at every level. If you are a working professional, you have had to navigate a new work force. If you have a family, you have had to learn how to maintain relationships, tolerate extended, extreme doses of proximity, and possibly train yourself to become an educator/parent/working adult. And all of that excludes the health implications with which you may or may not have been managing.

These circumstances have beat all of us down. But this isn't the first time in history humanity has been tested. Generations before have endured war, times of raging illness, famine, and depressions, and the list could go on. You may have a history of mental or physical illness that you have learned to live with, or with which you are still struggling to cope. Perhaps your child battles a mental or physical handicap or illness. The point is that struggle is nothing new. Yes, the last several months have been extraordinarily challenging, but we are not the first to contend with extraordinary circumstances.

We as humans, as women, and as leaders have a proud legacy of resilience. Defined as the capacity to recover quickly from difficulties or the ability of an object or substance to spring back into shape, resilience is the stuff of recovery. It is the muscle we need to emerge from trials, darkness, loss, grief, and the mire that is life. It is essential, intrinsic, and accessible. However, it requires a conscious decision on our part to access it and put it into practice. It is born of discipline, conditioning, repetition, and determination.

Before Jessie made her historic win on American Ninja Warrior, she was in active recovery. A torn ACL, MCL, and meniscus had sidelined her opportunity to compete in 2015 as well as put her career as a stunt woman on hold.

"I was stuck doing boring conditioning and needed something to inspire me during the 12-month recovery period," she said. "It wasn't just about Ninja Warrior. It was about getting strong enough to prevent injuries in the future. I was amazed to see how as I increased my strength, I got so much better at everything. Things that seemed hard or impossible became easy."

Her victory run didn't start from a place of strength, but of injury, weakness, and a commitment to recovery. Your victory run may feel out of reach today. You may be battered and broken and on the sidelines. Good news. You're exactly where you need to be.

You can't win if there is no battle. Victory requires adversity. You can't rise unless you begin at the bottom. In Romans, Paul writes, "Not only that, but we rejoice in our sufferings, knowing that suffering produces endurance, and endurance produces character, and character produces hope, and hope does not put us to shame, because God's love has been poured into our hearts through the Holy Spirit who has been given to us" (Romans 5:3-5, ESV).

I know you're tired. I understand how weary the journey can be. I've been knocked down. I have stared into an abyss of darkness, frozen in the absence of light. Hopelessness can induce a paralysis of the spirit that seems unbreakable, a chill upon your heart that feels impenetrable. I implore you to trust me when I say that you will move again. Your heart will keep beating. You will have a tomorrow.

How do I know? Beyond the very fact that I'm vertical, writing these words on the page, your future is assured in scripture. The God who created the heavens has also created a survival mechanism and instilled it within your soul. It's up to you to position your spirit, your body, your heart, and your mind to access it.

RESILIENCE

Your position is critical. Think of a sprinter. They begin every race in a crouched position, pushing off the starting blocks. A common analogy is to think of the legs like coiled springs. If the legs are straight, the springs are extended and can't deliver much power. However, when the legs are bent, they are ready to bounce into action.

There's more to it than a simple bend of the knee, however. Elite runners aim to have the proper angles and alignment so as to optimize their launch. According to Aaron Ellis, a seasoned high school track coach, it's easy to spot novice runners, as they tend to miss out on the full advantage of their starting position.

"On the first few steps out of the starting blocks, most untrained sprinters have a natural tendency to pop straight upwards, thus defeating the point of using blocks," says Ellis. "Trained sprinters learn to stay low for the first ten meters—known as the drive phase—taking powerful strides to transition into their acceleration phase."

There's power when you are down low. There is momentum to be gained when you know how to position yourself. The key here is training, discipline, and conditioning. If you are ready to go, to spring into action, you must train your mind. You must shift your perspective when it comes to the adversity that you are currently or will one day encounter. While this will yield a wealth of positive outcomes, there are three specific takeaways that will manifest in your life upon doing so.

First, you will be less of a target for the enemy. Think back to the obstacle course. When you are conditioned, when you have studied the obstacles and know what you will encounter, you will be better equipped to avoid, deflect, and overcome each one.

Second, you will be healthier. From your physical and mental condition to the status of your relationships, expect marked improvements when you commit yourself to a regimen. This may include spiritual disciplines like scripture study and prayer, physical disciplines like mindful eating and exercise, or mental disciplines like stress management and regular positive interaction with others. There's no one-size-fits-all routine to attain resiliency. Your situation is as unique as you are and will require personalized plans, choices, and actions. However, regardless of the content of your plan, your commitment to it will inevitably lead to enhanced health and well-being.

Finally, anticipate greater access to the Kingdom. In times of adversity and hardship, it can seem as if God, His promises, and His strength are unreachable. This is not His desire or His design. As you bring yourself and your life into alignment, you will feel Him and hear Him in ways that you may have not in a very long time, if ever.

As you journey through this book, I hope you gain a greater understanding of not only the concept of resilience, but its manifestation and application in your life and heart, here and now. I hope you feel a sense of renewal and strength. Most of all, I hope that you gain a sense of self-determination to see this season through, take stock of your struggles, and resolve to rise above those things that could so easily take you down. It's time for you to reclaim the life God has created for you. It's time to get up.

But before you do, let's pray for strength, wisdom, and insight for the journey. To borrow the words of the Apostle Paul:

RESILIENCE

Asking God, the glorious Father of our Lord Jesus Christ, to give you spiritual wisdom and insight so that you might grow in your knowledge of God. I pray that your hearts will be flooded with light so that you can understand the confident hope he has given to those he called—his holy people who are his rich and glorious inheritance. I also pray that you will understand the incredible greatness of God's power for us who believe him. This is the same mighty power that raised Christ from the dead and seated him in the place of honor at God's right hand in the heavenly realms (Ephesians 1:17-20, NLT).

Amen.

chapter
1

AIN'T I A WOMAN:
RESILIENCY IS INHERENT

"You formed my innermost being, shaping my delicate inside and my intricate outside, and wove them all together in my mother's womb."
—PSALM 139:13 (TPT)

"If the first woman God ever made was strong enough to turn the world upside down all alone, these women together ought to be able to turn it back, and get it right side up again! And now they is asking to do it, the men better let them."
—SOJOURNER TRUTH

The year was 1851. In London, the Great Exhibition took place at the Crystal Palace, showcasing the wonders of the burgeoning Industrial Revolution. In San Francisco, a major fire destroyed nearly 2,000 buildings, and Dr. John Gorrie patented a refrigeration machine.[1] In Akron, Ohio, at the Women's Rights Convention, a

---

1   https://www.onthisday.com/date/1851/may. Accessed February 20, 2021.

small, seemingly unassuming woman delivered an extemporaneous speech that would become one of the most revered in history.

About one month later, Marius Robinson, editor of Ohio newspaper *The Anti-Slavery Bugle*, published the first version of the speech. While it did not include the phrase itself, Sojourner Truth's address would come to be known as the "Ain't I a Woman" speech. Her words electrified the women in attendance and have continued to do so for generations of women around the world:

> *That man over there says that women need to be helped into carriages, and lifted over ditches, and to have the best place everywhere. Nobody ever helps me into carriages, or over mud-puddles, or gives me any best place! And ain't I a woman? Look at me! Look at my arm! I have ploughed and planted, and gathered into barns, and no man could head me! And ain't I a woman? I could work as much and eat as much as a man—when I could get it—and bear the lash as well! And ain't I a woman? I have borne thirteen children, and seen most all sold off to slavery, and when I cried out with my mother's grief, none but Jesus heard me! And ain't I a woman?[2]*

Over 150 years later, her words resonate with us, as we can only imagine what this amazing woman endured. Many leaders, like you, likely regard her speech as iconic, even more so when one considers the life, trials, and grit of the orator. Born into slavery in 1797 as Isabella Baumfree, this living portrait of resiliency was once sold with a flock of sheep for $100 to a cruel man, John Neely. A harsh, violent man, he would frequently beat her. Around 1815, she and a man

---

2 https://www.nps.gov/articles/sojourner-truth.htm. Accessed February 20, 2021.

named Robert fell in love and had a child. He was subsequently sold, and the two never saw each other again. In 1826, she escaped with her infant daughter but had to leave two children behind.

Over the years, she continued to encounter trials and hardships, including the loss of a child. But on June 1, 1843, she committed her life to Christ and abolitionism, and she changed her name; from then on, Isabella Baumfree would be known as Sojourner Truth. She chose that name to testify the hope that was in her.[3] Throughout her career in advocacy, she shared stages with the likes of Frederick Douglass and Harriet Tubman, working tirelessly for human rights.[4]

So how did she go from being sold with sheep to becoming one of the most esteemed advocates in American history?

Resiliency. This woman was resiliency personified.

Defined as the capacity to recover quickly from difficulties or the ability of a substance or object to spring back into shape, resiliency facilitated Truth's shift from tragedy to promise, from being silenced to being heard. Her inner strength was not happenstance and most certainly was not a result of a positive environment. Like a flower that breaks through concrete, Sojourner pressed through tremendous difficulties and blossomed for all to see. Her capacity to overcome, keep moving forward, and never give up came from within. It was intrinsic. She was born with it. And so were you.

---

3   https://www.loc.gov/exhibits/odyssey/educate/truth.html. Accessed February 20, 2021.

4   https://www.biography.com/activist/sojourner-truth. Accessed February 21, 2012.

Psalm 139:13 (TPT) reads, "You formed my innermost being, shaping my delicate inside and my intricate outside, and wove them all together in my mother's womb."

You are a glorious masterpiece! The spirit of God resides within you. It is woven into your DNA, and it is something that no one can ever take from you. Therefore, by design, grace, and love, your resiliency is inherent. Even in the darkest moments of your life, you have a well-spring of strength within, positioning you to lead yourself and others well. Awareness is only the first step; one must also choose to access it in order to flourish in this life. Likewise, the efficacy of your leadership is dependent on your capacity and willingness to tap into the Divine that resides within you.

THE SHAPE OF YOU

I love few things in life more than a day by the water with friends and family. Be it an ocean, a pool, lake, or creek; you name it, I love the feeling of the warm sand in my toes, the squeals of laughter from the kids around me soaking in the sun, and the gentle lapping of waves against the shore.

And what would a day on the waterfront be without a beach ball? Keep-away, dodgeball, and volleyball all showcase that rubber or plastic sphere in all its glory. But put it in water, try to push it beneath the surface, and you'll learn a lesson or gain a perspective that may just change your life forever.

Why? Because not even the strongest person can keep it down for long. The push back you feel is the buoyant force of the water at work. The air inside the ball works against the water to raise the ball to the surface again and again and again. Even if the ball is squeezed, once released, it will return its original shape. That ball is resilient. The ball will always win.

If air can keep a ball afloat, just think about what the presence of the Kingdom of God inside you can do. It does not matter what is pressing upon you from above or the sides; His presence makes you buoyant in the wild waters that make up this thing we call life. Wild waters indeed!

That does not mean that you will not encounter adversity. Chances are, as you have climbed the ladder of leadership, you have encountered opposition along the way. Rest assured, you will face more. Scripture guarantees it. In John 16:33 (MSG), Jesus says, "In this godless world you will continue to experience difficulties. But take heart! I've conquered the world."

This presents a dichotomy—one that is also reflected in nature. Without gravity, we would all float away—people, animals, cars, water, and even the atmosphere itself. But the intrinsic mass of earth generates the gravity necessary to ground us. Think about the beach ball. Its buoyancy only becomes apparent when it is being pushed through the water's surface, and the force of the air inside the ball encounters the force exhibited by the water.

Your personal degree of resilience or buoyancy will only be revealed in the face of adversity and opposition, which, as John 16 says, you will inevitably face. Without adversity, there is no need to demonstrate strength. Without trouble, there is no need to access the well of resilience woven through every strand of your DNA.

One of my favorite superheroes is Captain Marvel, who debuted in 1968 using the moniker Ms. Marvel. Several iterations later, Carol Danvers assumed the title and is likely the version with which you and I are most familiar. Carol Danvers as Captain Marvel rescued Iron Man from certain death in *Avengers: Endgame* before putting on a stunning display of ferocity in the final battle with Thanos. With near-invincibility, she shouldered the gauntlet containing the six puissant infinity stones, which had previously eradicated half of all existence in the Universe, contributing to the epic victory of good over evil.

What I love most about this character, however, is not her fighting or flying; it is the fact that she was born a human, yet when she encountered a blast, she acquired her powers. Without that explosion (adversity), she would have remained a fighter pilot, there would have been no plot, and I would have been forced to reevaluate my superhero preferences.

You can't win if there is no battle. The extent of your strength only manifests when you face challenges. Therefore, if you are genuinely committed to realizing the scope of your resiliency, you have to adjust the paradigm through which you experience and perceive adversity. Rather than fearing it or running from it, learn from it. Grow from it. Let it strengthen and sharpen you.

AIN'T YOU A WOMAN?

In one of her many speeches, Sojourner once referenced Eve from the Garden of Eden, saying, "If the first woman God ever made was strong enough to turn the world upside down all alone, these women together ought to be able to turn it back, and get it right side up again!"

Women have a special degree of resiliency, overcome struggle and hardship, and dig deep for the strength to keep walking. In her book, *My Sister's Keeper*, Jodi Picoult says, "The human capacity for burden is like bamboo—far more flexible than you'd ever believe at first glance."[5]

You may be experiencing trials at this very moment that make it difficult to remember who you are and Who resides within you. Perhaps you're questioning your role as a leader, wondering if you are equipped or able to guide others. Everyone encounters seasons like that. It doesn't mean you are a weak person or one without hope. It merely means you need to be reminded of who and Whose you are.

When Eve ate that apple and, as Truth says, "turned the world upside down," her choices brought upon womankind what we know as difficulty in childbirth. Even so, our God gave us the amazing capacity to give birth and recover well from the process of birth.

If you are a mother, I'm sure you probably recall what those contractions felt like as they progressed and grew stronger and stronger. But I bet you can also remember the moment you held your baby for the first time. In a split second, your agony became elation. The pain you felt all but disappeared within the weight of the love you held in your arms. What I recall, thirty-plus years later, is not the pain

---

5   https://home.hellodriven.com/50-resilience-quotes.html. Accessed February 12, 2021

of giving birth, but the joy of giving birth to my beautiful daughter, Lauren. The capacity to immediately react in love after the arduous task of labor is resiliency—your resiliency. It's not something you created. It's been within you from the start.

Sojourner Truth faced insurmountable odds her entire life. Eve experienced the shame of her sin and the pain of the fallout. You may have experienced the loss of a parent, a marriage, a child, or a job, and the list could go on. Yet if you're reading this, you have something in common with both of these women. You are a survivor. Truth made it through the darkness with purpose; Eve survived a hard delivery in the wasteland. Whatever you have experienced, you have made it this far because the capacity to keep going—your resiliency—has never changed or wavered. You are a woman. You are God's chosen helper and daughter. He created you to not only survive but also to thrive in this world no matter what.

In those moments when the pain is too sharp, the loss is too piercing, or the shame is too consuming, close your eyes, breathe deeply, and remember that He is with you, empowering you not just to endure but to overcome. You were made in the image of the almighty Creator. His Kingdom is within you, and there is nothing you can't overcome.

chapter
2

FOR THE GOOD:
RESILIENCY RENEWS PERSPECTIVE

"And we know that God causes everything to work together for the good of those who love God and are called according to His purpose for them."
—ROMANS 8:28 (NLT)

"Although the world is full of suffering, it is also full of the overcoming of it."
—HELEN KELLER

"Disability is not something we overcome. It's part of human diversity."
—HABEN GIRMA

I love that we celebrate high school graduation. At that point in our young lives, it is usually the most significant accomplishment we have. I still remember my 500 fellow graduates, all in red, and navigating my way to the platform through the grass in heels to receive my diploma.

For those who chose to pursue higher education, we soon realized how ill-prepared we were for adulting in those challenging environments. I have great admiration for those who have beaten the odds and received degrees. Only you know what it took to receive that diploma, and your story of accomplishment inspires me. There are other stories of resilience and achievement that leave me similarly in awe.

When Haben Girma graduated from Harvard Law School, not one, not two, not three, but four world leaders not only knew about her accomplishment, but extolled her diligence and herculean achievements. She received accolades from President Barack Obama, President Bill Clinton, German Chancellor Angela Merkel, and Canadian Prime Minister Justin Trudeau.

From my chair, merely getting into Harvard Law merits a lifetime achievement award of some kind. With about a 12 percent admission rate, the students who enter the program are the best of the best.

Haben is most certainly in that category. But there's something even more remarkable about her completion of the coursework at Harvard Law. When she graduated, she became the first deafblind person to do so. She is now leading as a human rights lawyer, working to advance disability justice. She released a memoir, *Haben: The Deafblind Woman Who Conquered Harvard Law*. Haben is more than a poster child for resilience.

Her story opens with a 12-year-old Haben being told she is failing classes due to missed assignments. In the teacher's office, she realizes that the assignments had been written on the board or given orally from across the room. She couldn't see them or hear them; therefore, she didn't do them. At that moment, she realizes if she were to succeed in a sighted, hearing society, she would have to go above and beyond every other student in every possible way. It was a shift in perspective that set her on a journey of academic excellence and influence.

I deeply admire the courage and tenacity Haben possesses, which helped her overcome the physical challenges she dealt with. Clearly, there is something for those who have the ability to see to glean from her example.

It is interesting that our perspective dictates so much of how we interact with the world and those around us. Defined as the way you see something, it is derived from a Latin root, meaning to look through or perceive. Every variant of the word has something to do with looking. Leadership is contingent on one's perspective, as it impacts the way you see those you work with and for as well as the manner in which you manage others.

The Bible has much to say about the views we take in, where we should be looking and where we shouldn't. 2 Corinthians 4:16-18 (TPT) reads:

> So no wonder we don't give up. For even though our outer person grad-
> ually wears out, our inner being is renewed every single day. We view
> our slight, short-lived troubles in the light of eternity. We see our dif-
> ficulties as the substance that produces for us an eternal, weighty glory
> far beyond all comparison, because we don't focus our attention on what

is seen but on what is unseen. For what is seen is temporary, but the unseen realm is eternal.

It's far too easy to focus on our troubles, failures, weaknesses, and tragedies. I know I have done it more than I would like to admit. When I do, two distinct things happen. First, if I am focused on the negative, I can't focus on the truth. The truth is that Jesus has already overcome every trial and injustice and loss with which I am wrestling. Once I allow myself to focus on problems, I lose sight of the truth. Who I am and what I have been called to do moves outside of my periphery.

This leads to the second consequence—I get stuck. Not only am I not looking for a way to move forward, but my capacity to interpret the world around me becomes so compromised that I may choose to do nothing and rather wait to be rescued. If resiliency is directly correlated with buoyancy, as discussed in chapter one, it cannot co-exist with stagnation. If we want to lead well, this is where we must be certain that our perspective is in line with His Truth.

So, what's the solution? We must shift our perspective. Rather than perceiving our difficulties as burdens threatening to take us out, we could consider them to be substances producing an eternal, weighty glory. Instead of viewing life and the world around us through a microscope, dissecting each component to the point of exhaustion and paralysis, we need to start looking through a telescope.

FORGET HINDSIGHT

As Haben Girma says, "Hindsight may be 20/20, but 20/20 is not how I experience this ever-surprising world." We can look over our shoulders all day long and consider all the would-haves, could-halves, and should-halves and stay in the exact same place. Or worse, if we're looking behind us, we may miss what's in front of us, whether it's an opportunity, new relationship, or obstacle that we won't be able to avert because our eyes are looking in the wrong direction. We don't have time to course-correct, and mistakes or worse can occur. This can spell disaster when you are not only responsible for your own course, but that of others.

Abraham's wife, Sarah, made some hasty decisions that led to negative consequences because her perspective had been thrown off. In Genesis 16, we read that Sarah had not been able to have children and offered her servant to Abraham so he would have a child. The fallout of this decision is just what you'd expect. Animosity grew between Sarah and her servant, Hagar, who ultimately ran away before an angel told her to return to Sarah.

I have known so many women and families who have struggled to have children due to infertility, miscarriages, or other heartbreaking circumstances. In particular, each woman experiences and reacts to these struggles in different ways, but the pain is almost always a visceral, sharp, cutting pain. I can only imagine how Sarah must have felt. In her culture and time, a woman was considered a failure if she could not produce an heir for her husband. Beyond that, she longed to have a baby of her own to hold and love. Her heart ached to know the tender love of mother and child. Perhaps this is why she resorted to an extreme that had dire consequences for everyone involved.

RESILIENCE

Does this mean Sarah was a bad person? Of course not! She was human. She was a woman with maternal longings and emotions. The problem arose when she allowed her emotions to dictate her perspective. Emotions have a way of painting a very different picture than what is portrayed in the Word of God. The promise that had been given to her apparently drifted from her site, and in place of it, it appears that all she could see was desperation. Had her eyes been trained on what was to come, perhaps she would have been able to trust in God's provision. Not long after Hagar's son, Ishmael, was born, the Lord appeared to Abraham and promised to make him into a great nation. He also said that Sarah would have a child within the year.

At this, Sarah laughed. What a human response! We get the sense that it was more of a "yeah, right, that isn't going to happen" kind of chuckle. At times, it seems like I'm looking in a mirror. How many times have I been told that great things would happen, but my perspective was so skewed, it sounded almost laughable to believe in a promise of something good? To the cynical, the promises of God can become comical. God was faithful, and she gave birth to Isaac within the year.

In the end, Sarah was blessed with a child, but I think it is important to note that several people were needlessly hurt along the way. As leaders in particular, we may not realize the impact that our actions and decisions will have upon those around us. Nothing we do is in a void. Our choices have repercussions and will either be a blessing or a burden to others, all of which are magnified when we occupy a position of leadership. Everything we do will trickle down to the betterment or detriment of those we lead.

A NEW NORMAL

Lately, many mental health professionals have said that we should hear and focus less on our susceptibility to harm and more on our ability to rebound from adversity when it comes our way. There's no point spending all of your energy trying to avoid problems. Not only is it exhausting, but it's also impossible. You will encounter hardship. You will encounter challenges. How you come through those challenges is a test of your resilience and a demonstration of your ability or inability to adapt. As we study the lives of those who managed to thrive during the pandemic, we will notice one key commonality—the ability to pivot.

The more graceful the pivot, the more beautiful the dance. The beauty of being able to adapt and pivot is the purity of our focus and the clarity of our perspective.

I applaud the countless professional women who had to learn to dance overnight. They were suddenly called upon to be teachers, chefs, inventors, and organizers in addition to their already numerous roles. They rearranged their entire lives. They learned to pivot, and they danced well.

CREATIVITY COUNTS

When we view life as full of potential and possibilities instead of problems, we then have the headspace to adapt and develop creative solutions. We have already stated that without adversity, there is no resiliency. That being said, what if we viewed the roadblocks and hurdles in life as opportunities for previously undiscovered solutions?

RESILIENCE

I'm sure you've heard that "necessity is the mother of invention." When the hurdles of life interrupt our norm, frustration isn't our only option. We can choose to create.

Case in point, I have a design background that emerged over the years. I believe part of this development was coaxed out of me as a young girl because of what I did not have. Growing up with four other siblings on a teacher's salary meant that we lived on a tight budget. When you don't have a lot of discretionary income, the focus is on necessities rather than niceties.

Like most young girls, I had a Barbie doll. Thanks to the commercials, I learned about the amazing Barbie house, and naturally, I longed for one of my own. I knew that it wasn't a possibility, so I set out to craft my own Barbie mansion from whatever I could get my hands on. It wasn't long before my sisters and friends asked me to build one for them as well. Looking back, I see that if I had responded to the "problem" differently instead of setting out to solve it, I would have missed the discovery of a creative solution.

History is full of creative individuals whose innovation was key to their strength. Many of these women are well-known leaders, occupying significant chapters in history that have subsequently shaped countless lives. Helen Keller is one of the most well-known leaders and symbols of resiliency in history. While she was born with sight and the ability to hear, she lost both at an early age and was blind and deaf for the rest of her life.

Her parents, desperate to help their daughter adapt and survive, took her to specialists all over the country and were eventually connected with Anne Sullivan. Anne, a teacher who also struggled with vision problems, moved into the family's home and began to try to teach Helen how to interact with her silent, dark world.

Nothing worked. Racked by temper tantrums, the young Helen was nearly uncontrollable, and Anne was making little progress. So, she got creative. She and Helen moved into a small cottage on the family's property, away from Helen's parents and those who tended to coddle her instead of teaching her. Over time, the two connected, and one day, while running water over Helen's hand and spelling W-A-T-E-R over and over, something clicked. Soon, Helen was touching objects, demanding to know the letters. It had worked. Anne had broken through. Helen and Anne were life-long companions, and Helen left behind a legacy of advocacy and community activism.

The running water was a simple solution. But it was creative. It was effective. Romans 8:28 (TPT) says, "So we are convinced that every detail of our lives is continually woven together for good, for we are his lovers who have been called to fulfill his designed purpose."

God cares about the tiny details of our lives. He can use them to bring us to moments of breakthrough. What's more, He can and does use them to help us shift our perspectives and see things a little differently. He is the one who enables us to make small course corrections along the way. Haben Girma discovered at the age of 12 that she would have to make additional overtures to succeed in school. Anne Sullivan realized that she needed to change the environment in which she and Helen worked.

These small changes led to significant shifts in perspectives that generated a spirit of resilience within these remarkable women. What are the small changes you need to make today to shift your perspective? Are you looking through a microscope at what has come before or through a telescope at what is on the horizon?

Take time today to lift your eyes. Consider that there are possibilities that you haven't yet seen, and trust God to lead you to new places with new perspectives and opportunities to not only rebound but to abound. These are the leadership traits needed for us if we want to be catalysts for change in our society.

chapter
3

THE SPACE BETWEEN:
RESILIENCY RESHAPES SUFFERING

"Dear friends, do not be surprised at the fiery ordeal that has come on you to test you, as though something strange were happening to you. But rejoice in as much as you participate in the sufferings of Christ, so that you may be overjoyed when his glory is revealed."

—1 PETER 4:12-13 (NIV)

"Suffering in its simplest form comes in the space between what we thought would be and what is."

—KATHERINE WOLF

"**M**y personality has always been woven through with a certain amount of grit," said Katherine Wolf in an interview with Authority Magazine. "It's certainly a combination of nature and nurture, but it's not truly activated until real struggle comes."

For Katherine, that struggle came from a massive brainstem stroke due to an AVM, a rare brain malformation. The catastrophic stroke should have taken the 26-year-old's life. Miraculously, she survived, but her life was changed forever. One moment she had been a healthy newlywed with a six-month-old baby. The next, she was fighting for her life. And the next, she was turning her suffering into blessings.

It's been nearly 11 years since the stroke. During that time, she and her husband have written two books, spoken all over the country, and launched a non-profit ministry and camp called Hope Heals and Hope Heals Camp to, as Katherine put it, "encourage anyone struggling to show up for a life they didn't sign up for."

The truth is that most of us will experience that feeling at some point or multiple points in our lifetimes. We will encounter the loss of loved ones, the loss of jobs, illnesses, injuries, betrayals, and the list could go on. Suffering is not a probability; it is a certainty.

Scripture tells us as much. 1 Peter 4:12-13 (TPT) reads, "Beloved friends, if life gets extremely difficult, with many tests, don't be bewildered as though something strange were overwhelming you. Instead, continue to rejoice, for you, in a measure, have shared in the sufferings of the Anointed One so that you can share in the revelation of his glory and celebrate with even greater gladness."

This passage, penned by Peter, was a letter to Christians, instructing them on how to live in a world where they would inevitably be persecuted for their faith and assuring them that regardless of the pain they experience on this earth, their eternity with God was secure.

Perhaps the most profound point of this passage, however, is found in the first verse, which says, "Therefore, since Christ suffered in his body, arm yourselves also with the same attitude, because whoever suffers in the body is done with sin" (1 Peter 4:1, NIV).

Let's unpack that a bit. First, this verse reminds us that Christ suffered. Suffering was the entire reason He was born. He was sent to take our punishments, to shoulder our iniquities, and to suffer in our stead.

It's easy and almost natural to feel alone in the midst of our own pain. Loss and grief frequently lead us to isolation, convinced that no one could possibly understand what we're going through. Those feelings are without merit because they stem directly from the enemy, who is a master at twisting even the very words of God for his vindictive purposes. If he can isolate us, we are less likely to resist his agenda.

Peter must have had some insight into this as he reminds the Christians that they are, in fact, never alone, regardless of the suffering they may be experiencing. He calls attention to the fact that Christ knows what it is like to hurt. He sees every tear you cry, every beat of your broken heart, and every dream that has slipped through your fingers. Hebrews 4:15 (NLT) says, "This High Priest of ours understands our weaknesses, for He faced all the same tests we do, yet He did not sin."

There is something cathartic about dwelling on this truth when you are suffering. If you are going to dwell on something, let it be truth. As leaders, we face difficulties unique to our position, and we can be tempted to think that no one else understands our situation.

In moments where I have been through betrayal, I have clung to this verse, and it has brought me great comfort.

A SAVIOR WHO SUFFERED

We serve a Savior who is intimately acquainted with grief and pain—not by accident but by an intentional, divine design. In Isaiah, we read the prophecy of the suffering Messiah to come.

> *He was looked down on and passed over, a man who suffered, who knew pain firsthand. One look at him and people turned away. We looked down on him, thought he was scum. But the fact is, it was our pains he carried—our disfigurements, all the things wrong with us. We thought he brought it on himself, that God was punishing him for his own failures. But it was our sins that did that to him, that ripped and tore and crushed him—our sins! He took the punishment, and that made us whole. Through his bruises we get healed (Isaiah 53:3-5, MSG).*

If we can truly accept the fact that Jesus understands what we are going through, our entire concept of suffering will change. Resiliency allows us to reframe our pain. It enables us to see that there is a purpose in our afflictions.

Katherine Wolf has found purpose in trials that would be insurmountable to most. "My story, as hard as it was, was, in fact, full of incredible possibility and unmerited advantages, and I didn't want to waste it," she says.

The Bible is full of women and men who have suffered and demonstrated astounding resiliency through their struggles. These lessons can teach us more than a hundred leadership seminars could even come close to doing! There's so much to learn from women like Ruth and Naomi, who experienced tragedy after tragedy. Naomi's husband died, leaving her with two sons and their wives. Then, both of her sons died, making her daughters-in-law, one of whom was Ruth, widows.

Understandably, Naomi was devastated. The Bible says she was bitter. Not wanting to keep her son's widows away from the chance of living a full life, Naomi was determined to return to her home-town and leave her daughters-in-law in Moab, where they lived, so they could find new husbands and start over. Ruth refused to stay. In the midst of her own grief, she was determined to remain by Naomi's side.

> But Ruth said, "Don't force me to leave you; don't make me go home. Where you go, I go; and where you live, I'll live. Your people are my people, your God is my God; where you die, I'll die, and that's where I'll be buried, so help me God—not even death itself is going to come between us" (Ruth 1:16-17, MSG).

It's striking how Naomi thinks of the happiness of her daugh-ters-in-law amid her tremendous loss. Likewise, Ruth is concerned with the welfare of her mother-in-law despite having just lost her husband. Both women demonstrated astounding grace through their suffering.

DEFYING THE ODDS, SURVIVING THE PAIN

We've all experienced some degree of suffering. No one's experience or reaction to it is identical; however, everyone who suffers has a Heavenly Father who sees and cares. Not only does He see and care,

He provides. The story of Ruth is a beautiful example of redemption. I have seen in my 60-plus years of life that although some things are not reversible, everything is redeemable. Even the most dire and bitter circumstances will change with Heaven's intervention.

In World War II, the relentless Japanese assault in the Philippines forced U.S. forces to retreat to the Bataan Peninsula. There, nurses from the U.S. Army Navy and Nurse Corps were among the first women to encounter combat conditions. Over the course of four months, in the sweltering heat, humidity, and acrid dust storms, they erected cots and makeshift medical facilities and treated over 6,000 soldiers.

Seventy-seven of these nurses, who called themselves the "Battling Belles of Bataan," were ultimately captured and sent to a Japanese internment camp where, despite brutal conditions and the threat of diseases like malaria and dysentery, the women kept their spirits up and continued to work. They established a four-hour workday, relieving each other if and when they became too weak to work.

Remarkably, all 77 women survived. Upon their liberation, they continued to work, treating the soldiers who had rescued them. It is one of the most magnificent stories of suffering, resilience, and survival from the war. By maintaining a sense of order, camaraderie, and focus, they survived the unsurvivable.

CELEBRATE CONTINUOUSLY

It's no small thing to put a smile on your face when you are staring down what seem like insurmountable odds. Whatever storm you are facing right now, rejoicing may very well be the last thing you feel like doing. Yet scripture tells us, "Rejoice always, pray without ceasing, in everything give thanks; for this is the will of God in Christ Jesus for you" (1 Thessalonians 5:16-18, NKJV).

It's one thing to read those verses and understand them with your head; it's another thing altogether to allow those words to penetrate your heart. I have been in places of pain so great; rejoicing wasn't merely something I didn't feel like doing, it was something I felt like I was unable to do.

Articulating the potential positive outcomes of our trials gives us the necessary hope and peace of mind to not only withstand the pain but to grow from it. Celebration and worship amid suffering is essential if restoration is to occur. The form of rejoicing He encourages us to participate in is worship. I have seen what happens when I open my mouth and declare the goodness of my God amid extreme heartbreak. If we are going to fight for anything, shouldn't it be the right to praise the name of our glorious Savior?

There is something liberating when you open your mouth and proclaim His name that breaks off oppression when it feels like it is smothering you. I have shouted the name of Jesus at the top of my lungs when I have been in the deepest valley. Worship is not just a temporary relief valve to make one feel better in the moment; it is a lifeline. It resets perspective, and when we engage in it with everything we have, strength is garnered from it. It is how we access His grace, and consequently, how we obtain grit.

I knew a family who learned their father had cancer, and they decided to throw a party. They had a "Tribulation Party," during which they prayed for healing with their loved ones. He ended up pulling through, all the while rejoicing despite the dire circumstances.

Like this family, Ruth and Naomi, and Katherine, we will face circumstances that will cause pain. We will suffer. But we do not have to despair. In the dark places, our resilience manifests. When we can find the good in the bad, our strength grows. Our suffering is no longer a burden we have to carry on our own; instead, it is an opportunity to grow closer to God, acknowledge our vulnerabilities and shortcomings, and become stronger.

Consider your suffering. Are you hurting today? Are you holding on to the pain of the past? I challenge you to take time to think on or even write down your circumstances, their origin, and most importantly, the good things that have emerged or you hope will emerge in time. And then, even if you don't feel like it, pray a prayer of gratitude. Ask God to reveal the purpose of your pain. Implore to understand how your suffering will equip you to become a stronger leader. Once you know where it is coming from and what it is for, suffering will take on a new meaning. It will no longer be a one-sided road to defeat; instead, it will become an opportunity to grow, develop compassion, and fully surrender your heart and soul to the One who created them.

chapter
❧ 4 ❧

THE ONE LESS TRAVELED:
RESILIENCY IS PATHWAY

*"Don't sin by letting anger control you. Don't let
the sun go down while you are still angry."*

—EPHESIANS 4:26 (NLT)

*"Two roads diverged in a wood, and I–
I took the one less traveled by,
And that has made all the difference."*

—ROBERT FROST[6]

It's hard to find the words to describe the year 2020. The COVID-19 pandemic wreaked havoc around the globe. Economies were crushed as businesses were not only temporarily shuttered but closed down completely. Healthcare facilities were over-run and under-supplied, and tragically, as of this writing, nearly two and a half million people have lost their lives worldwide.

---

6   Frost, Robert. *The Road Not Taken*. https://www.poetryfoundation.org/poems/44272/the-road-not-taken. Accessed February 21, 2021.

RESILIENCE

Against this backdrop, the struggles facing many minorities due to systemic racism in our nation for centuries were brought to the forefront with the slayings of George Floyd and Breonna Taylor. While thousands of peaceful protests took place across the country, inevitably, some areas experienced violence and vandalism.

It was a sobering reminder of the racial divide that was written into law less than 70 years ago. In Montgomery, Alabama, busses were divided into black and white sections. While other laws stated that no one could be forced to give up their seat, it was custom for the drivers to have authority to ask a black person to give up their seat for a white person.

On December 1, 1955, Rosa Parks was riding one of those busses. While she was sitting in the designated black section, a white man couldn't find a seat in the white section, so the bus driver demanded that Parks move.

She refused.

Interestingly, just twelve days earlier, she had encountered that same bus driver. After paying her fare, she refused to go to the black entrance. The driver tugged at her sleeve, and she ended up getting off the bus altogether. December 1 was another story. Her refusal to leave her seat led to her arrest. She would later be fined $10, plus another $4 to cover court costs.

Her actions ignited a bus boycott that lasted over a year. On November 13, 1956, the Supreme Court ruled bus segregation to be unconstitutional. Parks lost her job and endured harassment for years but became known as "the mother of the civil rights movement."

In her memoir, she wrote, "People always say that I didn't give up my seat because I was tired, but that isn't true. I was not tired physically . . . No, the only tired I was, was tired of giving in."[7]

Ms. Parks had two choices that day, two paths. She could have gone the easier route and given up her seat. Or, she could dare to stay true to her convictions and refuse to move. One was more familiar than the other. It was less risky. But it would have made no difference in the fight for civil rights. Her choice could have jeopardized her life. In many ways, it did. She endured harassment for years following the incident; however, she also facilitated a historic step in the fight for equality. It was a bold decision that made her a leader and role model to so many others also striving to be seen and equally valued as human beings.

While we may not be able to identify with Ms. Parks' experience in totality, there is one element that we encounter multiple times per day—choices. Ms. Parks had two—get up, or stay seated and face the consequences. Every day as leaders, you and I also have to choose the path we will traverse. In particular, when and where we find ourselves facing a challenge, there are often only two paths in front of us from which we can choose. Resilience is one such path. The other is that of resistance. Whereas resilience is defined as having the capacity to bounce back or recover, resistance is defined as inflexibility and rigidity, which can be more detrimental than we realize.

Each pathway is representative of thought patterns. The path of resistance is familiar because it represents our default position, one

---

7   https://www.history.com/topics/black-history/rosa-parks. Accessed February 20, 2021.

we can easily navigate on our own without help from God or others. When you occupy a position of leadership, it is tempting to assume this posture. Erroneously, we convince ourselves that we don't need assistance from anyone, not even God. Resistance doesn't require humility; resiliency is founded upon it. It is an unfamiliar path that requires dependence on God to find it and traverse it.

To further compare and distinguish the two from each other, consider this: The path of resistance shouts, "I am justified in my attitude!" Meanwhile, the way of resilience is inquisitive and eager to explore the redemptive process.

More often than not, the path of resistance leads to detriment, while resilience leads to development.

CIRCUITRY ISSUES

Most people have patterns and standard responses to external stimuli. They react the same way over and over to certain personalities or situations. Said actions are preceded by thought patterns ingrained within the brain, thus triggering the same behavior patterns. In fact, the way we feel is determined by the way we think, not the other way around.

Dr. Caroline Leaf explains that the pathways in the brain resemble the branches of a tree. As we experience certain things, process them, and then behave accordingly, we develop and establish circuitry patterns within the brain. According to Dr. Leaf, "Thoughts are real, physical things that occupy mental real estate. Moment by moment, every day, you are changing the structure of your brain through your thinking."[8] That means that each time we accept a negative thought as truth, and each time we rehearse that negative thought, the more it gets carved into our psyche and the more it is reinforced in our minds. This is how strongholds are formed.

We tend to take in life in a sensory manner—sight, smell, sound, and touch. All this information floods our nervous systems and triggers a response, usually an emotional one. This is by design. When we are in threatening situations or facing rejection or injustice, we instinctively feel hurt or angry. Anger feels very powerful, which is often what we need. As cortisol, a hormone, floods our system, the fight or flight response kicks in. God created us this way for our protection. He equipped us with intrinsic survival skills, and it's helpful when we are faced with certain situations

When I was in school, I was a cheerleader. I was a proud cheerleader. And if there's one thing that is essential to every cheerleader, it's her pom-poms. One day, at a game, I realized that my pom-poms were not where I left them. I didn't completely panic, but I was highly concerned. And then I spotted them with a group of guys who were about to light my pom-poms on fire! Without a second thought, I marched over to them and reclaimed what was mine.

Looking back, it's a bit of a silly story. At the moment, however, it was a deal—a big deal. Today, I realize that it wasn't just about rescuing a set of pom-poms; it was about reclaiming my peace and joy.

---

8   Caroline Leaf, Switch On Your Brain: The Key to Peak Happiness, Thinking, and Health. https://www.goodreads.com/author/quotes/773964.Caroline_Leaf. Accessed February 21, 2021

I cannot begin to imagine what Rosa Parks thought and felt that day on the bus. I admire the fact that she did not give in to fear or react in anger. She stood her ground by staying in her seat. She made a statement that she was a human being just like any other rider of any other color. She reclaimed her peace. Rather than continue to say nothing, acquiescing to a racist society's irrational demands, she chose to take a different path. That choice, her resilience, changed the world. Her posture of resilience inspired an entire movement.

EVEN WHEN IT HURTS

It's easy to default to what's familiar, particularly in times of distress. When the world around us goes crazy, it takes a lot of determination and focus to interact with our circumstances differently. It feels more natural and requires less energy to revert to what we know.

For example, if someone betrays us or hurts us, it's much easier to blow up or blow them off rather than seek to understand where they're coming from, or at the very least, explore our feelings of rejection. We can spend so much time waiting for other people to make things right or do something that will give us a sense of peace. We want our anger to be justified by their admission of wrong.

That's a toxic, slippery slope. We can't control what other people do, how they think, or how they regard us. As leaders, in particular, we must safeguard our reactions to others while adjusting our expectations. We must accept that despite the guidelines and structure we put in place, they are not things to which we can force others to adhere. What we can control are our actions and attitude. We can control the path we choose to take. We can choose the path of resilience over the path of resistance.

Anne Frank has become a symbol of resilience, perseverance, grace, and optimism for millions worldwide. Born into a Jewish family in Germany in 1929, Anne received a red-and-white-plaid journal for her 13th birthday. In it, she wrote, "I hope I will be able to confide everything to you, as I have never been able to confide in anyone, and I hope you will be a great source of comfort and support."

Less than one month later, on July 6, 1942, she and her family went into hiding from the Nazi regime. For the next two years, she wrote faithfully in her diary about everyday life, the fear of capture, and plans for her future. Her last entry was made on August 1, 1944. Soon after, her family was captured and sent to concentration camps. Anne and her sister went to Bergen-Belsen while her parents went to Auschwitz.

By the end of the war, only her father was still alive. Friends of the family went to the Franks' hiding spot where they found Gestapo papers and Anne's diary. *Anne Frank: The Diary of a Young Girl* was initially published in Dutch in 1947. Since then, it has been translated into 70 languages, with over 30 million copies sold. In it, she wrote, "I still believe, despite everything, that people are really good at heart."[9]

Anne had two pathways from which to choose while in hiding. She could have been bitter and angry at those who were persecuting her family, or she could opt to take the much more challenging path of optimism. Page after page, her diary is not one of a girl bent on revenge or clinging to anger. It is full of hope, humor, and resilience.

---

9   https://www.britannica.com/biography/Anne-Frank. Accessed February 19, 2021.

She didn't let anger make her rigid or resistant. She was like a willow tree, bending gracefully in the face of a storm.

THE TOXICITY OF ANGER

Ephesians 4:26 (NLT) says, "Don't sin by letting anger control you. Don't let the sun go down while you are still angry."

Anger can be a treacherous pathway. Those who are angered easily and frequently are rigid. They are stuck somewhere. Perhaps they are replaying a trauma over and over. Maybe they are attempting to reconcile a betrayal or failure of some kind. Regardless, those who become rigid can't grow or move on. That's not to say that anger is always a bad thing. What can be toxic is when that anger is left to simmer and penetrate your heart and mind.

There will be many moments of fear and anger in your life. That's inevitable. But you have a choice as to whether you will allow those things to break you or bend you. Resiliency will enable us to bend and then return to our original form once the storm has passed. Resistance will break us. It makes us brittle and fragile. It leaves us in a state of perpetual brokenness, within which we miss out on life.

Here's the catch: You can't achieve or maintain resiliency on your own. You have to surrender your pain and let the Holy Spirit cast light upon your path, guiding you step-by-step to healing and freedom. As we walk, compassion will well up inside. We will begin to see the power of truth, experience restoration, and rest in hope and peace.

That's not to say it will be easy. We've already established that resiliency is by far the more challenging of the two paths before us.

It will seem unfamiliar until our mind becomes renewed, our old circuitry and patterns of thinking re-routed, and new characteristics developed.

We don't know what tomorrow will bring. Our normalcy has been disrupted, and our daily routines have been derailed. And now, we have a choice to make. We can succumb to frustration, anger, and lack of control. Or, we can choose to see that perhaps God is allowing us to tread a new path. He dwells within you, and, yes, He is the way to heaven, but He is also the way to life here and now.

chapter
5

WHEN WE SAY YES:
RESILIENCY IS IGNITED BY OBEDIENCE

"This is why I remind you to fan into flames the spiritual gift God gave you when I laid my hands on you. For God has not given us a spirit of fear and timidity, but of power, love, and self-discipline. So never be ashamed to tell others about our Lord. And don't be ashamed of me, either, even though I'm in prison for him. With the strength God gives you, be ready to suffer with me for the sake of the Good News."

—2 TIMOTHY 1:6-8 (NLT)

"And so I discovered that it is not on our forgiveness any more than on our goodness that the world's healing hinges, but on his. When he tells us to love our enemies, he gives along with the command, the love itself."

—CORRIE TEN BOOM[10]

---

10 https://www.crosswalk.com/faith/spiritual-life/inspiring-quotes/40-powerful-quotes-from-corrie-ten-boom.html. Accessed February 19. 2021.

RESILIENCE

Between 1943 and 1944, Corrie Ten Boom's family, friends, and neighbors saved approximately 800 Jews and other refugees from the Nazi regime. When they were betrayed, the Ten Booms were arrested and sent to concentration camps. Corrie's father died after just ten days. Corrie and her sister, Betsie, were sent to Ravensbruck Concentration Camp, which was almost unbearable.

While there, Corrie and Betsie shared the love of Jesus with the other prisoners, many of whom became Christians. Betsie died at Ravensbruck, but Corrie survived. Following her liberation, Corrie spent the next thirty years traveling to over sixty countries, sharing how the love of God is greater than our greatest pain and how God's love can give us the power to forgive our enemies.[11]

Her story shared striking similarities to that of Paul's when he wrote the second letter to Timothy. Like Corrie, Paul was imprisoned. He knew his death was imminent, hence the sense of urgency within his correspondence. He urged Timothy to continue to grow in his faith and reminded him of his obligation to be bold in sharing Christ, to stir up his God-given gifts. He charged him to be obedient to the call placed on his life.

Both Corrie and Paul are impeccable examples of resiliency. In the direst circumstances, they not only chose to but were able to fan the flames of their spiritual gifts. Why? Because they were prepared, bold, and obedient.

---

11 https://www.corrietenboom.com/en/information/the-history-of-the-museum. Accessed February 20, 2021.

2 Timothy 1:7 (NLT) reads, "For God has not given us a spirit of fear and timidity, but of power, love, and self-discipline."

Good leadership requires the type of resiliency that only emerges in the presence of obedience. When we respond to God's call, He equips us with the courage and wherewithal to answer it, but it is up to us to listen, obey, and take action.

THE FORCE OF FORGIVENESS

Before we can be bold for Christ, sharing His love and His message of hope, we have to rid ourselves of bitterness and past offenses we haven't forgiven. As Ephesians 4:31-32 (NIV) states, "Get rid of all bitterness, rage, and anger, brawling and slander, along with every form of malice. Be kind and compassionate to one another, forgiving each other, just as in Christ God forgave you."

This is easier said than done. To forgive is one of the most extraordinary feats of strength one can demonstrate. I say this because it is challenging for us to forgive ourselves, let alone forgive others. It requires something more than superhero strength.

One of the greatest struggles in my life was forgiving an aggressor. When I was ten years old, a family friend molested me on several occasions. I admired this person, which made it that much easier to be manipulated. To this day, that individual has yet to apologize or even acknowledge their actions. However, I can confidently say that I am completely restored and have forgiven him.

Statistics tell us that there's a high probability that you or someone you know has been through something similar and quite possibly worse. However, my story is what I have to offer in hopes of helping you in the way that Jesus helped me to overcome. Our stories may differ, but the sacrifice of Jesus is the same.

Our misunderstanding of what forgiveness truly is, in my mind, is part of what makes it a challenge for us to comply with. We know that Jesus commands us to forgive. But forgiveness is no small thing. It can often feel arduous to the point where we give up. This was the way I thought for many years as I waited for the perpetrator to make amends. In fact, I thought that my forgiveness of him was reliant upon his apology. That was until I realized that it was predicated upon something entirely different.

I recall reading in Romans 5 the comparison between the first Adam's transgression and the second Adam's (Jesus') gift of grace and forgiveness. It parallels their actions and the cause and effect on all humanity. Amid these passages, a light came on for me.

> *Now, there is no comparison between Adam's transgression and the gracious gift that we experience. For the magnitude of the gift far outweighs the crime. It's true that many died because of one man's transgression, but how much greater will God's grace and his gracious gift of acceptance overflow to many because of what one man, Jesus, the Messiah, did for us (Romans 5:15, TPT).*

The first Adam in my life had caused some devastation; however, when I began to consider how much more significant the actions of the second Adam—my Savior—were, I had to make a choice. Which Adam was I going to allow to rule in my life? I made a conscientious choice to enable the work of the cross to be my cause to forgive him as Jesus had forgiven me. You do some things by feeling, and there are other things you can only do by decision.

Hebrews 12:24 (TPT) goes on to encourage us further, "And we have come to Jesus who established a new covenant with his blood sprinkled upon the mercy seat; blood that continues to speak from heaven, 'forgiveness,' a better message than Abel's blood that cries from the earth, 'justice.'" The blood of Jesus speaks of greater things than justice or vengeance.

You have likely had an Adam in your life. You can choose to focus on what they did or focus on what the second Adam did. At some point in our lives, each of us will have to decide which is greater: the sin of the other person against you or the sacrifice of Jesus for you.

Forgiveness has nothing to do with reconciliation, nor is it predicated on the other person changing their ways. It is about you changing your outcome, being free from the burden of carrying the offense. This is how you stop allowing someone who has taken from you to continue to rob you of more life. Forgiveness halts the progression of bitterness.

Jesus paid for the sins of all humanity, which is good news because we are all equal opportunity offenders. We are all capable of causing harm. If His blood was sufficient to pay the ransom for all sin, then we must avoid the temptation of "villainizing" our fellow humanity. This means we remove them from this category of being unforgivable and put them square with us on the same ground as being forgivable.

Not every act is easy to forgive. On the other hand, the forgiveness every act requires has already been paid for by the sacrifice of Jesus.

So, this is our starting point. While in excruciating pain, Jesus, dying on the cross, beheld those who had maliciously put Him there. His response was, "Father, forgive them, for they do not know what they do" (Luke 23:34, ESV).

This is a remarkable statement for us to consider in the midst of our own pain. We follow His example and ask God to first extend His mercy and His forgiveness to us. I cannot explain what occurs when we do this, but afterward, it is less difficult for us to extend our forgiveness.

Mercy is one of our superpowers. We are to love mercy in the same manner that God does, and through humility, our hearts will have the capacity to offer unrestrained forgiveness and mercy. Proverbs 3:3 (NKJV) reads, "Let not mercy and truth forsake you; bind them around your neck, write them on the tablet of your heart."

NOT BY MIGHT

If resilience is ignited by obedience and obedience is predicated on forgiveness, one might conclude that this linear path is relatively easy to follow. One would be mistaken. To face adversity and come out standing requires a degree of spiritual resiliency that we cannot evoke on our own; we have no choice but to rely on God's strength and the skills with which He has endowed us.

Dunamis is a Greek word meaning strength and skill. It appears approximately 120 times in the New Testament. While the term means power, it isn't referring to human strength. It is relegated to instances of divine, supernatural power, typically associated with signs and miracles. For example, Matthew 22:29 (NIV) says, "You are in error because you do not know the Scriptures or the power of God."

The word appears again in Matthew 24:30 (NIV): "Then will appear the sign of the Son of Man in heaven. And then all the peoples of the earth will mourn when they see the Son of Man coming on the clouds of heaven, with power and great glory."

This power is intrinsic to God. When we become reborn in Him, so, too, does it reside within us. As leaders, it is critical to first acknowledge God's power within us and learn how and to choose to access it regularly. You will face adversity particularly as your influence grows. You will inevitably be thrust into scenarios, some of your own doing, others not, that require supernatural strength not only for your survival, but also for the sake of those whom you serve. There is an element of courage involved in being willing to forgive, and it is this very type of courage that helps us face those situations and individuals and exercise forgiveness when and where it is needed.

FANNING THE FLAMES

"With the strength God gives you, be ready to suffer with me for the sake of the Good News" (2 Timothy 1:8, NLT).

Paul offers no sense of false security in his letter to Timothy. Quite the opposite. Whereas one might assume that obedience to God as demonstrated through bold testimony, a willingness to forgive and be forgiven, and surrender to the power of the Holy Spirit would result in a peaceful life, Paul knew first-hand the fallacy of that idea.

RESILIENCE

Throughout his 35-year ministry, he was jailed multiple times. While no one can be entirely sure how many times, it is clear that Paul suffered. During his second missionary journey, Paul cast a demonic spirit out of a woman who was a slave. Before this, her owners made a lot of money off of her. The demonic spirit's expulsion put an end to this, and they were none too happy about it. Enraged at their loss of their income-generator, they had Paul and Silas, his counterpart, thrown in jail. Ultimately, the two men spent less than a day in prison before a massive earthquake shook loose their chains.

When the jailer realized what happened, he was prepared to kill himself for losing all the prisoners. When that happened, Paul yelled out that they were still where they were supposed to be. Despite the opportunity to escape, Paul and Silas remained obedient. The jailer was so shocked by their behavior, he immediately asked what he needed to do to be saved (Acts 16:30, NIV).

It's a fascinating composite of faith, forgiveness, and obedience. Paul and Silas did not demonstrate bitterness towards their captor-keeper. They were so filled with the promise of God's faithfulness that there was no room to harbor resentment. Without a second thought, the two men resolved to stay obedient. These demonstrated acts of faith are like brushstrokes on a portrait of resilience. Perhaps the most monumental takeaway is the direct correlation between their actions and the jailer's desire to know Christ. Their obedience and spirit of forgiveness led to resilience, which forged a path directly to the throne room, to salvation itself.

As I consider the story of these two men in prison, I am struck by the use of song and speech. Before the earthquake released the chains, the Bible tells us that Paul and Silas were singing hymns so loud that the entire prison was singing along. It was their cry that stayed the jailer's hand before he took his own life. And it was their explanation of salvation that led the jailer to Christ.

Words have power. Yet adversity can lead to deafening silence. Shame is the language of timidity and fear. It convinces us to say nothing about Jesus. As a leader, your words and the delivery of them are imperative to your success. When you harbor shame or allow fear to diminish your voice, you are short-changing the leadership skills with which God has endowed you.

Take a look at Esther. Long story short, she was born and raised Jewish. King Xerxes ruled the kingdom in which she lived, and, following a fall-out with his queen, Vashti, he was on the hunt for a new bride. Esther was called to the palace with other girls from throughout the kingdom, where she quickly distinguished herself and eventually became Queen Esther.

Not long into her reign, one of the King's top advisors developed a vendetta of sorts against Esther's uncle, Mordecai. When Mordecai refused to bow down to Xerxes instead of God, his advisor, Haman, did not approve. He convinced the King to destroy Mordecai's people—all the Jewish people in the kingdom. The King agreed, not knowing that his queen was among the targeted group.

When Esther and Mordecai learned what was coming their way, Mordecai implored Esther to go to her husband and plead for their lives. Small problem—those who approached the King without an invitation could be killed. Esther had no invite, but she also had limited time to stop the coming genocide. She gathered her courage and faced the King. Ultimately, while the King couldn't lift the decree entirely, he asserted that the Jewish people could defend themselves, veritably giving them a fighting chance and preserving their population.

I can only imagine what must have been running through Esther's mind. First, there's the "no invitation leads to death" situation. Secondly, up to this point, her husband didn't even know she was Jewish. Thirdly, her uncle and fellow countrymen were counting on her—not for a handout or lower taxes; they were depending on her for their very lives.

Esther had to decide whether to be obedient to her God or allow fear to silence her. She opted to do what a good leader does—she relied upon the strength of her faith and took a risk on behalf of those she served. The result? Much like with Paul and Silas, her obedience led to salvation.

When we step out in obedience, there is a surge of boldness and resilience. Resilience transcends adversity. But it is up to us to choose. Corrie Ten Boom stated, "Forgiveness is an act of the will, and the will can function regardless of the temperature of the heart."

You may not feel like obeying God's call on your life right now. You may not feel like forgiving those who have wronged you. You may not even feel like speaking up. But obedience, boldness, and forgiveness aren't about feeling. They're about doing. They are action steps you can take regardless of your emotions.

Leaders like you must learn to heed the call of the present circumstance and not get lost in a tirade of emotion or indifference. You are already equipped with everything you need to face your adversaries and emerge a victor. Dunamis dwells within you. Prayerfully, implore the Lord to reveal it to you and guide you as you apply it. Over time, you will see that your obedience has not only served others, it has also made you stronger, more resilient, and more prepared for the next challenge you will encounter.

chapter

6

CALM IN THE STORM:
RESILIENCE CULTIVATES COMPOSURE

"So I'm not defeated by my weakness, but delighted! For when
I feel my weakness and endure mistreatment—when I'm
surrounded with troubles on every side and face persecution
because of my love for Christ—I am made yet stronger.
For my weakness becomes a portal to God's power."
—2 CORINTHIANS 12:10 (TPT)

"How very little can be done under the spirit of fear."
—FLORENCE NIGHTINGALE[12]

If the pandemic has taught us anything, it is the indispensability of our first responders. Day after day, nurses, doctors, and other healthcare professionals have put their lives on the line to care for COVID-19 patients. Without question, they are true superheroes.

---

12 https://www.goalcast.com/2018/02/08/inspirational-florence-nightingale-quotes/. Accessed February 19, 2021.

RESILIENCE

Throughout history, great tragedies have uncovered great heroes. After 9/11, the firefighters, police, and medical personnel's bravery was lauded for their bold efforts to save those trapped inside the towers.

In 2020, while COVID-19 ravaged the world, our first responders once again deservedly emerged as a bright light in a very dark, almost surreal landscape. Day after day, with or without the proper PPE or equipment, healthcare workers around the world put their lives on the line to care for COVID patients. They did so diligently, willingly, and compassionately.

They were resilient in the face of one of the greatest crises the modern world has experienced. In the chaos and uncertainty, they performed their duties with composure and the calm reassurance desperate situations demand. There is much leaders like you and I can learn from them—from their compassionate care to the organizational prowess such a crisis demands.

Steady actions and calm attitudes are practically synonymous with healthcare providers, particularly nurses. It is a proud legacy handed down since the profession's inception in the mid-1800s by "the Lady with the Lamp," also known as Florence Nightingale. Nightingale's professional prowess had distinguished her to the point that the British Secretary of War reached out to her and requested she put together a team of nurses and come to Crimea, where the hospital was severely under-staffed.

Within just a few days, Nightingale sailed to Crimea with 34 nurses in tow. When they arrived at the British base hospital in Constantinople during the Crimean War, nothing could have prepared them for what they saw. The water and the hospital itself were contaminated. Patients lay in their own filth while bugs and rodents scurried among them. Bandages, soap, and even water were in short supply. The conditions were so appalling, more soldiers were dying from infection than their battle wounds.

The situation would have shaken the most steadfast of individuals. But Florence remained calm, level-headed, and soon had every able-bodied person cleaning while she made rounds, at times in the dark holding only a lamp, to the wounded patients. Her attentiveness and care quickly earned her the nickname, "the Lady with the Lamp" or "the Angel of Crimea." The lamp she carried in the dark was symbolic of the resilience she carried within. Before long, her diligence, leadership, and calm but direct manner reduced the hospital's death rate by two-thirds.[13]

After the war, Florence, who was also a statistician, helped conduct a study, during which they discovered that 16,000 of the 18,000 deaths in the war were caused by infection and illness—not injury. Florence presented these findings to the Royal Commission, showing that the cleanliness protocol she had established in Crimea led to drastically higher survival rates. This information led to new sanitary protocols to be implemented in the army and beyond.

Lauded by patients, colleagues, and others, Nightingale was honored by the Queen of England with an engraved broach and $250,000. Nightingale used the money to found St. Thomas Hospital

---

13 https://www.history.com/topics/womens-history/florence-nightingale-1. Accessed February 19, 2021.

and the Nightingale Training School for Nurses. Her work elevated the nursing profession from one of obscurity and often disdain to a desirable career path for women across the socio-economic spectrum.

Throughout her life, she exhibited an enviable degree of self-discipline and composure under pressure. The longer she served the wounded soldiers, the stronger her resilience grew, and the more cultivated her composure became. Her capacity to evaluate a situation, identify a solution, and execute it successfully despite being in a war zone testifies to her steadfastness in the face of tremendous adversity. The power of resilience is the ability to maintain composure and subsequently uncover solutions in the midst of adversity.

Nightingale's degree of self-discipline is one to which we should aspire. Self-discipline denotes careful, rational thinking. It is the ability to think clearly with the wisdom and understanding that God imparts. Fear is a driving force in society today. It is the main subject of the evening news and the underlying premise of advertising and marketing. Fear often spawns confused thinking, irrationalities, and misunderstandings. Thoughts and speculations swirl in our minds when fear enters. This is why Christ calls us to healthy, orderly thought processes.

STRENGTH IN WEAKNESS

While Florence faced tremendous stress in the war-ravaged hospital, you and I also face stress and encounter trials that seem impossible to overcome. The truth is, that's the idea. We weren't created to muscle through problems and challenges on our own. Rather, we were created to rely on God and His power to help us face the darkness.

In 2 Corinthians, Paul writes, "So I'm not defeated by my weakness, but delighted! For when I feel my weakness and endure mistreatment—when I'm surrounded with troubles on every side and face persecution because of my love for Christ—I am made yet stronger. For my weakness becomes a portal to God's power" (2 Corinthians 12:10, TPT).

When we rely on the strength of our Savior, trials will not ruin us. They refine us.

What the enemy sends to destroy becomes a display of His glorious might, no matter how big or small, mundane or extraordinary. He is present in our everyday stress. When we are empty, He gives us His fullness. When we are mired in adversity, He enables us to develop resilience. If we trust in His strength, our strength grows accordingly. And as our capacity to get back up, move on, and keep trying despite any failures or roadblocks we encounter grows, our own composure is increasingly cultivated.

You may be wondering how this all plays out. Typically, when we encounter a threatening, stressful, or otherwise unpleasant situation, our fight or flight instinct flares up. That is our emotional response and should be heeded with great caution. If we rely solely upon our emotions or intuition to make decisions, we don't allow God to play into the decision-making process, and, more often than not, those choices fall through.

RESILIENCE

This is where we must make a shift from impulse to critical thought. When we take a beat and regain our composure, we will discover a sense of clarity that allows us to think clearly, be decisive, focus, and free ourselves of distraction. Once we achieve this, creativity can emerge, informing our problem-solving capabilities. If we manage to maintain the right perspective, we will have a vision in front of us, the Spirit within us, and wisdom granted to us.

The Bible is filled with scripture that can enable us to reevaluate and shift the paradigm from which we encounter and react to challenges and distress. In Exodus, when the Hebrew nation was being pursued by Pharoah and his formidable army, Moses assured the people to stay calm, saying, "The Lord will fight for you. You need only to be still" (Exodus 14:14, NIV).

In the book of Mark when the disciples were caught in a raging storm on the Sea of Galilee, Jesus diffused the situation. Mark 4:39-40 (NIV) reads, "He got up, rebuked the wind and said to the waves, 'Quiet! Be still!' Then the wind died down and it was completely calm. He said to his disciples, 'Why are you so afraid? Do you still have no faith?'"

There is not a tempest you will ever encounter that the Lord cannot stay. He will equip you to soothe your nerves, manage the sources of stress, and regain your composure.

It may seem uncomfortable or foreign to you to examine your personal level of composure, strength, or anger, but until you do, you'll never have a baseline. Don't be afraid to uncover or acknowledge your weaknesses. The best leaders are transparent and aware of their weaker areas so they can intentionally work to improve them. The one who can boast about their weakness is not insecure; they are honest.

Just like Florence Nightingale surveyed the daunting task of that dilapidated military hospital, a personal evaluation lets you survey your areas of strength and those you can improve upon. It is only through an honest assessment that you will develop a genuine aura of composure. In any moment of adversity, there are two things leaders take note of: the situation that is taking place in front of them, and the solution that is available to them. Resilient composure helps us to access the latter.

You don't have to do it alone. The Holy Spirit can guide you if you allow your heart to hear His prompting. Since He is the Spirit of power, we have confidence that He will enable us as we step out in obedience. Since He is the Spirit of love, we have empathy, which moves us into action to value those we serve. Since He is the Spirit of self-control, we respond with clarity and restraint.

chapter
7

NO MORE OFFENSE:
RESILIENCY IS LINKED
TO HUMILITY

"Good sense makes one slow to anger,
and it is his glory to overlook an offense."

—PROVERBS 19:11 (ESV)

"A man who is truly humble is not troubled when he is wronged."

—ISAAC OF NINEVEH[14]

History has always been punctuated with divisiveness, exclusion, and angry rhetoric. Even in the U.S.' relatively short period of existence, we have been engaged in multiple conflicts around the world and on our own soil.

Be it the advent of social media, the aggressiveness of certain political or social agendas, or the proliferation of news about absolutely everything every single minute of the day, society seems to be,

---

14 https://www.azquotes.com/quote/667713. Accessed February 19, 2021.

and in many places, is at a breaking point. It's as though the only thing everyone can agree on is that everyone else is offended by everything all the time.

That's a bit of an exaggeration, but only a bit. We are living in a tenuous moment in history. Be it masks, race, politics, health and safety, school, energy sources, and even diet, almost anything can be a trigger. Patience feels like a thing of the past—tolerance, like a pipe dream. And being offended is the new black.

Perhaps adding to the vitriolic energy is the lack of humility. Few of us seem ready or able to concede that we may not have all the answers. Rather, we have cloaked ourselves in our stances and opinions, and there is no room for negotiation.

It's an unhealthy way to live and could prove disastrous for our future or our kids' future. As leaders, we have a responsibility to temper the environments in which we circulate and command a presence. But before we can even think of diffusing situations that don't directly involve us, we must first get a handle on our own offendability, patience, and humility, because without those three things in check, our capacity for resilience will be feeble at best.

In 2 Corinthians, Paul writes, "But he answered me, 'My grace is always more than enough for you, and my power finds its full expression through your weakness.' So I will celebrate my weaknesses, for when I'm weak I sense more deeply the mighty power of Christ living in me" (2 Corinthians 12:9, TPT).

If Christ's power is at its optimal expression when we are weak, it stands to reason that we might want to admit that we do have weaknesses. But be cautious here. There's a difference between humility and insecurity. Insecurity says, "I can't do this." Humility says, "I can't do this alone."

When our weakness is clothed in humility, it is not debilitating; it is hospitable for the Holy Spirit to work His way in and through all the things we can't.

OFFENSE: MY KRYPTONITE

If resiliency has to do with bouncing back, if it speaks of recovery, then perhaps we should give some thought to the speed of recovery and what inhibits or contributes to this. I can speak from my own life and say that the main contributor to the speed of my recovery is the speed of my capacity to forgive. In other words, holding on to offense slowed down my ability to bounce back. The times I let go quickly and forgave my offender, my recovery time was always much quicker.

Speaking of speed, let's talk Superman. He's faster than a speeding bullet, leaps between tall buildings in a single bound, and is practically invincible, but there is one caveat—kryptonite. The phosphorescent space rock can take him down and make him useless. Knowing that the debilitating substance would likely occupy space on planet earth somewhere, he knew he had to find a way to avoid it. Our super-hero had to learn to detect kryptonite before the radiation powers unleashed their crippling effect.

Friend, you and I may not be vulnerable to a glowing rock, but we all have some version of kryptonite. From my observations, our weakness, our debilitation is offense. Just like kryptonite wasn't going anywhere, the issue of offense—being offended, offending others—will be a reality as long as we walk this earth.

We've all experienced it and the pain it evokes. Jesus warned us that being offended would be part of our human experience. Just like kryptonite, it can paralyze our lives. How do we truly know when we are offended? What does it feel like? Scripture gives a powerful analogy, "It is easier to conquer a strong city than to win back a friend whom you've offended. Their walls go up, making it nearly impossible to win them back" (Proverbs 18:19, TPT).

Imagine that you are the one locked behind those walls of offense. The wall represents a state of mind—isolation, distance from others. It may appear to be a fortress that will protect us from pain, but it provides only false security. Rather than being a place of safety, it is a place of harm. It is constructed with blocks of negative thoughts, and the mortar holding it together is anger. It is not a sanctuary; it is a prison.

When someone is serving a prison sentence, they are fed what the jailer chooses to feed them. The jailer is the enemy of our soul, and he feeds us the same bitter meal over and over again. Bitterness is often described in scripture as a root that springs up and defiles our lives. The root of bitterness warps our perspective of others. Over time, we perceive more and more people to be our offenders or potential offenders. This paranoia leads to a life of isolation and loneliness behind that wall, which is difficult, but not impossible, to dismantle.

In fact, I believe this is why Jesus warned us of the potential for offense, so that we could be prepared and less susceptible to the trap laid out for us. Is it possible to avoid falling prey to offense? The

Greek word for offense, skandalon, means trap and specifically points to the bait inside the trap. I believe that He was encouraging us to have a certain awareness, a poise of soul, an intentionality of heart, or a state of preparedness to take the bait. I also believe that we need to be aware of the triggers which are unique to us. I would even suggest that you prayerfully write them down so that you know what your version of krypotonite looks like. For example, my triggers tend to be when I am devalued or disrespected. Knowing this helps me to put on an attitude of love by clinging to the scriptures that help me avoid taking the bait.

I am the type of person who can be sensitive at times and vulnerable to offense. Knowing this about myself, I decided to explore how one could practically avoid being offended, getting caught in this trap. Being in ministry and around multitudes of people, the chances of being offended increases. In the thirty-plus years of being a pastor, I have had countless conversations in the lobby of our church. Needless to say, many people take the liberty of sharing their opinions on a range of topics, from how they felt about the worship songs to what they thought about my shoes. One never knows what someone will say, and I would find myself stung by criticism over things that truly did not matter, but hurt none the less. Therefore, I made it a point on weekends to walk in love, as Paul encourages us in Ephesians 6:10 to put on the armor of God. It was an intentional act that put me in a place of preparedness to love no matter what. What I discovered is that love is truly a forcefield. When I set my focus on loving others, critical words had little or no effect on me. In addition, I discovered a bonus benefit, a sense of humor!

On one particular weekend, I came to church sporting a new hairstyle. As expected, there were many comments and opinions about my haircut. I recall one woman looking at me in shock and uttering, "What have you done with your hair? It is way too short; the way you wore it before was much better!" Immediately, I reached up and patted her on the arm with a smile and said, "Don't worry, it will grow back." As she walked away, I laughed inwardly, knowing that response was a gift from the Lord. Instead of finding her comments to be hurtful, I found them to be humorous. I do not mean to suggest that this will apply to every situation, but we would be surprised how often this can be the case. In any event, love is a powerful force, and it is the fruit of our submission to the Holy Spirit. When we operate in that frame of mind, it opens our eyes to see things differently, which includes having a sense of humor! Joy is a byproduct of love, and being able to laugh at certain things is very liberating. The merry heart is not just a medicine; it is a preventive measure for offense.

We live in a highly sensitive world. There is a temptation for us to self-protect, particularly given the current climate where criticism has evolved into a cancel culture. However, we cannot allow potential hostility to rob us of resiliency. We need to be aware that the more we are concerned and focused on self, the more vulnerable we are to offense. Our reactions to offensive situations give strong indication of who is dominating our focus and the state of our heart. Love is not touchy or fretful, but those who live in a state of offense are highly sensitive. Love doesn't keep a record of wrongs, but those offended can recall the wrongs done to them in vivid detail. Being offended is not a neutral state of being, and it most likely leads to resentment and mistrust. When we are offended, we become locked in a viewpoint where bitterness distorts our perception.

Recall from chapter two the story in Genesis of Hagar, a servant to Sarah, Abraham's wife. Sarah couldn't have children, and though God had promised she and Abraham would, she took matters into her own hands and delivered Hagar to her husband's tent. Soon enough, Hagar was pregnant. And everything from that point went about as well as one would expect.

Once Hagar became pregnant, she flaunted her baby bump in front of Sarah, who was none-too-pleased and grew more bitter by the day. Deeply offended and conflicted, Sarah treated Hagar so badly that Hagar ran away. When an angel found her in the desert, she was instructed to return to Sarah. Knowing the misery awaiting her back at Abraham and Sarah's camp, she grudgingly acquiesced and returned to her former home, where she delivered a son, Ishmael.

It's fascinating to observe the interplay of humility, or lack thereof, and the degree to which each character offended and was offended. Sarah grew impatient for God to give her a child. She did not have or demonstrate humility and decided to play God. The repercussions proved to be pretty bleak for all parties involved.

Once pregnant, it was Hagar's turn to abandon humility. In so doing, she offended Sarah, who in turn offended Hagar. It was a vicious, unnecessary loop that played on repeat. While Sarah did eventually have a child, and Abraham ultimately did become the father of many nations, there were needless casualties along the way, all of which could have been avoided with a dash of humility and common decency.

It's hard to pick out a protagonist in this story, particularly between the two women. However, their story is a masterclass on the dynamics of offense and humility. God had more in store for them above and beyond their petty feud.

He has more for you as well. As a leader, you will make choices that impact others. You will have the option to base your decisions and actions on humility or your own pride. You can choose to interact with others in a manner that is offensive or not. Likewise, you can choose to be offended by the words and actions of others or be an example to those looking to you for guidance and leadership and rise above offensive statements or behaviors of others.

The trap of offense can be avoided. Default settings can be changed, but it takes time. When we become intentional about being ready to believe the best about others, we are grasping the power of unconditional love. We never lose when we love well with humility. We change, and our eyes are opened to abundant living. Most importantly, we please Him, and we look like Him.

chapter

8

FIERCE AND FOCUSED:
RESILIENCY CREATES STABILITY AND TENACITY

"So now, beloved ones, stand firm, stable, and enduring. Live your lives with an unshakable confidence. We know that we prosper and excel in every season by serving the Lord, because we are assured that our union with the Lord makes our labor productive with fruit that endures."

—1 CORINTHIANS 15:58 (TPT)

"The most difficult thing is the decision to act, the rest is merely tenacity. The fears are paper tigers. You can do anything you decide to do. You can act to change and control your life; and the procedure, the process is its own reward."

—AMELIA EARHART[15]

---

15 https://www.brainyquote.com/quotes/amelia_earhart_120929. Accessed March 3, 2021.

RESILIENCE

In 2012, gymnast Gabby Douglas became the first African American and first person of color of any nationality to win the All-Around gold medal at the Summer Olympics in London. She was the only team member to compete in all four apparatus (beam, floor, uneven bars, and vault). That same year, Team USA, dubbed the "Fierce Five," also claimed the team event gold medal. Following the games, Gabby encountered a few years of instability. She switched coaches multiple times, resulting in an inconsistent training schedule and lower scores in various competitions.

Yet her performances at various events secured her spot on the 2016 Olympic team. There, she helped the U.S. win a second consecutive team event gold medal, her third career Olympic gold.

While many questioned whether Gabby could rally and return to the Olympics, Gabby knew what she was capable of and what she needed to do to keep pushing her dream forward.

"Even if you have the talent, you still have to push yourself," she says. "I don't think dreams magically appear, that's why they're called dreams. But if you do want to make that dream a reality, then you have to push yourself. It takes a lot of hard work, and if you don't have the focus, then it's going to be all the harder. If you have a big dream, it takes all of the above to achieve it: passion, the focus, and the effort."[16]

Gabby's resiliency did not come from her previous wins or accolades. It didn't come because of endorsement opportunities and media appearances. Her resiliency was born of the inner stability

16 https://www.azquotes.com/quote/1579553. Accessed February 20, 2021.

and tenacity she began developing in childhood. Her formative years were hallmarked by poverty and homelessness.

In an interview with Deseret News, Gabby recounted the struggles they had experienced. "I was very young, so I don't remember (the details), but my mom and my siblings said it could be cold at times; we ate off the floor, off napkins," Douglas said. "It was my motivation to accomplish my dreams. My family and I had to overcome a lot to get where we are today."[17]

Her circumstances were less than ideal. Her opportunities were limited. But she knew who she was and what she was all about.

"God has given me this amazing God-given talent, so I'm going to go out and glorify His name," she says.

Gabby didn't grow up with financial stability or socio-economic privilege. Yet her heart was steady and sure, anchored in Christ, propelled by the kind of tenacity that takes one from the streets to the Olympic podium. "No one is going to feel sorry for you, so you have to go out there and be fierce," she says.[18]

STRENGTH TRAINING A SOLID FOUNDATION

When you determine that a life of resilience is one you wish to lead, you can't sit still and expect blessing, strength, and transformation to just happen. You have to work for it. You have to train your mind and

17 https://www.deseret.com/2016/8/10/20593594/u-s-olympian-gabby-douglas-intense-christian-faith-and-its-profound-role-in-her-quest-for-success#the-united-states-gabrielle-douglas-trains-on-the-balance-beam-ahead-of-the-2016-summer-olympics-in-rio-de-janeiro-on-aug-4-2016. Accessed February 20, 2021.

18 https://www.azquotes.com/quote/800768. Accessed February 19, 2021.

heart. Colossians 1:11 (NIV) encourages us to be "strengthened with all power according to his glorious might so that you may have great endurance and patience."

Leadership requires strength. Strength requires a strong foundation made of solid material. You'd never build a house with crumbling bricks or rotting wood. The entire structure would collapse on such a feeble foundation.

Yet when it comes to the rest of our lives, we tend to rely on less-than-reliable sources for our building materials. Opinions and gossip have largely replaced facts and truth. While it's perfectly normal to have opinions, problems arise when we confuse opinion—which is defined as a belief or judgment that rests on grounds insufficient to produce complete certainty—with truth.

Social media has given opinion a great big world in which to roam wild. With millions of anonymous users, commenters, critics, influencers, and viewers sitting behind their screens, espousing what they think about something and finding solidarity with others who agree, there are hardly enough agreed-upon "facts" upon which we can build anything, much less a solid structure.

Strong opinions result in weak convictions. You cannot have weak convictions and strong faith. Today, it seems like more people have opinions about the Word of God than convictions. That's incompatible with a life lived in the fullness of God. When you read the Word, there are essentially two reactions you can have—obedience or opinion.

Imagine if you were Gabby Douglas up on the balance beam. The judge just said that you wobbled and will get a deduction. If you respond with something like, "In my opinion, I made an artistic flourish," how far do you think you're going to get? You can't argue with the rule book. The technical execution for every apparatus and skill is spelled out in detail. As a gymnast, you either complete each element as detailed in the guide, or you don't and will face deductions.

The Word of God doesn't exist so we can argue with it. It's not up for negotiation or broad interpretation. It is what it is. It is truth, and it is crucial for our well-being.

If it is optional for you, it can never be transformational. We need epiphany if we are to improve our foundation. It's time to replace opinions about the Word with obedience to the Word.

"He will be the sure foundation for your times, a rich store of salvation and wisdom and knowledge; the fear of the Lord is the key to this treasure" (Isaiah 33:6, NIV).

The Word of God resides in a place of authority, not subjectivity. It is unchanging. Likewise, God is our stable, strong foundation that does not waver and isn't malleable to the opinions and whims of popular culture. If we are to eliminate uncertainty and fear of our worldly endeavors—family, relationships, career, finances, health, etc.—we must embrace a fear of the Lord.

This doesn't mean to be scared of Him. Rather, fear of the Lord is born out of holy reverence. If we are to be respected in our positions of leadership, we must begin with our own heads bowed to the One who reigns in total authority. The Word has not lost its authority, but we are living in an age in which many people have lost their appreciation of it. When we assume a mantle of holy fear and reverence towards God, we will discover solid ground beneath our feet. Over time, our stance will become increasingly secure as we become more like Him—loving what He loves, hating what He hates. In humble awe and respect, our fear of the Lord makes us empty, receptive vessels for wisdom and discernment. These are the solid materials upon which you continue to build a life that honors Him, while leading in a manner that reflects Him.

A STRONG CORE

Once your foundation is secure, it's time to tend to your core. Any trainer will emphasize the importance of this because your core muscles hold everything else together. From your running stride to your posture and alignment of your spine, the muscles of the core work in concert to maximize your performance and enhance your balance and stability.

Here's the thing—you're not going to get those abs you want or the core strength you need by sitting on the couch watching Netflix with a bag of Doritos. Just as you would work your arm and leg muscles, so, too, must you work the muscles that comprise your core.

If you were in a gym, I'd suggest weighted crunches, roman twists, and maybe a turn or ten on the ab wheel. When it comes to your spiritual and emotional well-being and your position in leadership, you strengthen your core through faith, as is shared in the book of James.

Dear brothers and sisters, when troubles of any kind come your way, consider it an opportunity for great joy. For you know that when your faith is tested, your endurance has a chance to grow. So let it grow, for when your endurance is fully developed, you will be perfect and complete, needing nothing (James 1:2-4, NLT).

Notice that while faith is the key to growth, faith only grows when it is tested. In the same way that a muscle requires resistance in order to become stronger, our faith will necessarily have to meet adversity if it is to become stronger.

Perhaps one of the greatest, or at least most prevalent, struggles our faith encounters on a daily basis is the myriad of influences we are subjected to. Be it online, on TV, or in social circles, work, or school, we are constantly being pulled in different directions, which generates inner-turmoil.

But God promised us a life of abundance, not confusion. It's easy to get lost in the milieu of words constantly thrown at us. However, we have a stabilizing mechanism at our disposal.

Solomon told his son to treasure and obey God's commandments, to "tie them on your fingers as a reminder. Write them deep within your heart" (Proverbs 7:2-3, NLT).

When an actor memorizes a script, the character becomes part of who they are. They begin to act, speak, and even think like the person on the page. The more they internalize the language of their character and the world and plot in which they reside, the more convincingly they can portray them.

When Solomon tells his son to write God's commandments on his heart, he is encouraging the same thing. When you read scripture and commit it to memory, it becomes part of who you are. Like an actor studying the intricacies of a character, when we pore over the Word of God and commit to memorizing it, the nuances, details, and characters become a part of who we are. They invade our heart, strengthening our core from the inside out.

Once the Word is alive inside of us, we put it into practice. Actors don't memorize scripts they never intend to perform. Why, then, would you read and internalize the transformative Word of God and never share it with anyone? Most leadership positions require some form of continuing education to enhance skills, remain current, and continue to grow as a professional.

Why would you not invest just as much time and attention into your spiritual growth and development? Commit to the memorization and meditation of scripture. Create a routine that puts you in the Word of God consistently. Over time, as your core strengthens, you will notice a change in your posture, your endurance, and your resiliency.

As James 1:22-25 (NLT) says, "But don't just listen to God's word. You must do what it says. Otherwise, you are only fooling yourselves. For if you listen to the word and don't obey, it is like glancing at your face in a mirror. You see yourself, walk away, and forget what you look like. But if you look carefully into the perfect law that sets you free, and if you do what it says and don't forget what you heard, then God will bless you for doing it."

SECURE IDENTITY

"My speed is a gift from God, and I run for His glory. Whatever I do, it all comes from Him," says Allyson Felix, multiple-time Olympian and gold medal winner.[19]

It's one thing to be strong and steady. But unless you know who and Whose you are, your physical gains, which are temporary at best, will do little to satisfy your soul and help you achieve the purpose for which you were created.

Allyson Felix is one of the most decorated Olympians, having smashed records and claimed title after title. However, she never loses sight of her true identity and source of strength.

"The most important lesson that I have learned is to trust God in every circumstance," says Allyson. "Lots of times we go through different trials, and following God's plan seems like it doesn't make any sense at all. God is always in control, and he will never leave us."[20]

Allyson doesn't find or base her identity on winnings or rankings. Rather, she is rooted deep within the infinite love of Christ. He is her solid foundation. His love strengthens her core, and His mercy has given her a new name.

God wants you to have the same assurance as Allyson does, that your every step is being watched and cared for. He wants you to experience His love in such abundance that you can't keep it to yourself, and it spills over into the lives of those who work with you, whether beneath you or even above you.

---

19 https://playersbio.com/allyson-felix-quotes/. Accessed February 18, 2021.

20 https://playersbio.com/allyson-felix-quotes/. Accessed February 18, 2021.

RESILIENCE

In his letter to the church at Ephesus, Paul writes that he prays for unlimited resources of God to infiltrate every part of the peoples' hearts and homes:

> *I pray that from his glorious, unlimited resources he will empower you with inner strength through his Spirit. Then Christ will make his home in your hearts as you trust in him. Your roots will grow down into God's love and keep you strong. And may you have the power to understand, as all God's people should, how wide, how long, how high, and how deep his love is (Ephesians 3:16-18, NLT).*

When we are rooted and grounded in His love, we possess an inherent strength and take part in a love that cannot be contained—a love whose breadth exceeds the measures of space, whose length exceeds the measure of time, whose depth exceeds the ability to be challenged, and whose height exceeds the reach of anyone and is beyond intellectual comprehension. It is a love that resides in a dimension that can only be understood as faith.

When we internalize this love and allow its roots to penetrate the depths of our soul, we discover the confidence and security we not only need to grow, but to love others better.

You get to decide. You can choose who and what determines your value. As you contemplate diving deep into the love of the one who invested so significantly in you, remember these words from Paul:

> *"So, my dear brothers and sisters, be strong and immovable. Always work enthusiastically for the Lord, for you know that nothing you do for the Lord is ever useless" (1 Corinthians 15:58, NLT).*

chapter
9

THE INERTIA OF EMPATHY:
RESILIENCE IS A CATALYST FOR COMPASSION

"Rejoice with those who rejoice, weep with those who weep."
—ROMANS 12:15 (ESV)

"I tell my story not because it is unique, but because it is the story of many girls."
—MALALA[21]

J esus wept" (John 11:35, ESV).

It's the shortest verse in the Bible but one of the most poignant. It reveals a side of Jesus often forgotten. We see His grief, His sense of loss, and the pain that accompanies the loss of someone you hold dear.

In John 11, we read the story of Lazarus, the brother of Mary and Martha. This Mary was the same Mary who anointed Jesus' feet with oil and wiped them with her hair. This was a family with whom

---

21 https://malala.org/malalas-story. Accessed February 19. 2021.

Jesus was close. When someone sent to word to Jesus that Lazarus was sick, they said, "Master, the one you love so very much is sick" (John 11:3, MSG).

Jesus' initial response to the news is surprising, if not confusing. Rather than heading straight to Lazarus, Jesus waits for two days to begin His journey. By the time He arrives, Lazarus has been dead for four days.

Upon His arrival, Martha runs to greet Him, saying that her brother would be alive if He had only been there. Mary later says the same thing before breaking down in tears.

"When Jesus saw her sobbing and the Jews with her sobbing, a deep anger welled up within him. He said, 'Where did you put him?' 'Master, come and see,' they said. Now Jesus wept" (John 11:34-35, MSG).

The tears seem a sharp contrast to Jesus' initial reaction, "'Lazarus died. And I am glad for your sakes that I wasn't there. You're about to be given new grounds for believing. Now let's go to him'" (John 11:14-15, MSG).

Perhaps, though, rather than view these two contrasting responses as a juxtaposition, consider them an intersection. Jesus' decision to wait had a purpose, yet Lazarus' death still grieved Him. And it is there—where grief meets purpose—that empathy is born.

There is a difference between empathy and sympathy. Defined as the ability to understand and share the feelings of another, empathy differs from sympathy. Sympathy is when one feels pity or sorrow for someone else's misfortune. Sympathy is to care at arm's length—not to keep people away, but because that's as close as one can get, not having experienced a trial like or similar to the one in pain. There is an intrinsic degree of distance in sympathy.

Sympathy is essential, and it is good. However, it does not incentivize us as empathy does. Whereas sympathy occurs vertically—looking down to the one in pain with pity—empathy is horizontal. It places us on the same plane, eye-to-eye with the bereaved, the sick, the jobless.

Jesus was empathetic. Just like Mary and Martha loved Lazarus and lost him, Jesus, too, loved him and lost him. When they wept, He wept.

But the story does not stop there. Sympathy and empathy are but two components of a progression that is set in motion by resilience. Before long, the act of being aware of another's struggle and identifying that struggle with your own creates inertia that leads to external acts of compassion.

Jesus did not merely weep with Mary and Martha and head home to mourn His dear friend. His empathy prompted him to act.

Jesus gazed into Heaven and said, "Father, thank you that you have heard my prayer, for you listen to every word I speak. Now, so that these who stand here with me will believe that you have sent me to the earth as your messenger, I will use the power you have given me." Then with a loud voice, Jesus shouted with authority: "Lazarus! Come out of the tomb!" (John 11:41-43, TPT).

The resurrection of Lazarus is the overflow of Jesus' empathy and compassion. It is that same compassion that motivated Him to leave Heaven and take on the form of a man.

And it was compassion that compelled Him to endure the suffering of the cross.

Many bystanders who watched Him suffer on that tree wondered why He didn't use His power to come down from the cross. They didn't realize that it was the power of compassion that kept Him on the cross. It was the ultimate expression of resilience—a catalytic expression of compassion that impacted all of humanity for all of time.

That, my friend, is the treasure of resilience. You, too, can experience the inertia of sympathy and empathy that leads you to compassionately impact the world around you. Resilience has never been a commodity you keep to yourself. It is intended to overflow, spilling into the lives of those around you.

Jesus is the perfect expression of this triumvirate—sympathy, empathy, compassion.

His compassion is not only a gift we receive; it is an ideal we should emulate. His perception of us, the assessment of our value, is utterly unconditional. Regardless of our mistakes, the many times we fall and fail, our value does not diminish in His eyes.

He knows and understands the carnal pain and struggle you and I experience every day. Before He was even born, Jesus' carnal suffering had been foretold. Jesus was fully aware of His mission from the beginning of time. He remained faithful to His ministry; He modeled resiliency in the face of adversity. And He suffered so that He could demonstrate empathy toward us—so that when we falter, even when we break—we have a Savior who understands and shares our feelings.

Isaiah 53:3 (NIV) says, "He was despised and rejected by mankind, a man of suffering, and familiar with pain. Like one from whom people hide their faces, he was despised, and we held him in low esteem."

Hebrews 4:15 (NLT) echoes that, "This High Priest of ours understands our weaknesses, for He faced all of the same testings we do, yet He did not sin." He is perfection in that He empathizes with us in our weaknesses, yet He did not give in to weakness personally. This shows us that we can still have empathy even if we haven't had the same experience. Moreover, like Jesus, we can allow that empathy to prompt us to action.

DEMONSTRATING EMPATHY

As of this writing, the U.S. has surpassed 500,000 deaths from COVID-19. That's 500,000 families who have been devastated, 500,000 families looking for absolution, 500,000 families who may be wondering where God has been in the midst of their pain and loss.

Herein lies an opportunity. With suffering all around us, we have a chance not only to put our past pain and loss in perspective, but also to share our battle wounds with others in distress. As Jesus did with Martha and Mary, this is a time to weep with those who weep and rejoice with those who rejoice.

The efficacy of our leadership is staunchly tied to our capacity to feel and demonstrate empathy. In an article from *Forbes Magazine*, Brandon Swenson states:

> *Having the ability to show respect, empathy, and care to those that follow you, are all attributed to being a great leader. Earning respect is*

crucial to a successful relationship with someone, while also showing that you care about their work or ideas. Being empathetic allows a leader to tap into the emotions of that individual to connect in a way that lets that person know you understand what it means to be in their situation.[22]

One of the most remarkable examples of empathetic, compassionate leadership began with a near-tragedy.

On October 2012, in Pakistan, 12-year-old Malala Yousafzai was shot in the left side of her head by a lone gunman.[23]

Malala was an outspoken advocate for education equality in her home country of Pakistan.

Many other people would likely have walked away from their causes following such a brutal attack. Malala chose otherwise.

"I knew I had a choice," said Malala. "I could live a quiet life, or I could make the most of this new life I had been given. I determined to continue my fight until every girl could go to school."

She did just that. Following the shooting, her speaking grew more passionate, more compelling, and more impactful. She was now speaking as one who had been persecuted for her convictions. Moreover, the very fact that she continued her advocacy was a powerful testament to the strength of her cause.

In 2014, she established Malala Fund, a charity committed to giving every girl the opportunity to pursue an education and a future

22 https://www.forbes.com/sites/brentgleeson/2016/11/09/10-unique-perspectives-on-what-makes-a-great-leader/?sh=532856fe5dd1. Accessed February 20, 2021.

23 https://malala.org/malalas-story?sc=header. Accessed February 19, 2021.

she chooses. That same year, Malala won the Nobel Peace Prize in December 2014, becoming the youngest-ever Nobel laureate.

A bullet brought this young woman to that intersection of purpose and pain. There, she discovered and adopted a mantle of empathy. Malala can now look directly into the eyes of girls who are suffering due to lack of opportunity, abuse, or fear and offer hard-won words of hope. And then, she can extend her hand and help. Her empathy has overflowed. Her life is one of compassionate care and action.

I can't help but see bits and pieces of myself within her story. I have made concerted efforts over the years to redirect my emotional energy so that bitterness wouldn't strangle my ability to fully live and drown out the possibility of good, the chance to use my experience to truly see others eye-to-eye, offering genuine understanding and care.

It's not always easy. Instinct wants to curse those who have caused me harm. I know how easy it is personally to harbor bitterness. But just as Malala chose to leave bitterness behind and turn her potential tragedy into a movement of hope, I have learned to exercise self-control, respond empathetically even to those who hurt me, and live a life that can be characterized as resiliency in action.

As a leader, you don't just bring your leadership skills to the table; you bring your whole self to every situation, whether you want to or not. You can't erase your past. Your scars aren't going to disappear, but you can use them. You can determine to bless those who have hurt you and bless those whom you serve by allowing your past to become a source of empathy. It won't be easy at first. It takes time to develop your mind and heart to put this kind of resiliency into action.

Be patient with yourself.

Above all, never forget your Heavenly Father, who knows all of your pain and has bigger dreams for your life. Just as Lazarus was left in the tomb for four days so that the glory of God may be revealed, whatever you are facing, have faced, or will encounter, God will use it for good. Not everything is reversible, but all things are redeemable. Your pain can have a greater purpose. Your life has meaning above and beyond anything you could imagine. Your experiences, good and bad, are blessings in that they will enable you to touch more lives, offering genuine, compassionate care. As you adopt a more empathetic approach to others, you will be more conscious of your reactions and will likely respond more calmly in the eye of the storm.

In moments of despair, we must cling to what we know to be true about walking through fires and trials. I know that pain and trauma can contribute to the building of character. It can make us more compassionate, empathetic, and appreciative of the good in our lives. I have learned that I can allow the force of pain to forge within me His character, and one of the most powerful traits we see in the life of Jesus was His compassion, His ability to empathize with those who were hurting. Each of these characteristics—their presence or absence within us—will define our leadership style and the degree of our impact upon others.

CULTIVATING COMPASSION

As you encounter challenges, accumulate scars, and fight your battles, you are essentially building an arsenal of experiences that moves you along the spectrum from sympathy to empathy. Once you can empathize with others, you can then begin to cultivate compassion, an essential attribute for Christians and leaders like you. Like we already established—inertia: one element leads to another.

Living in full resiliency means there is an overflow from our lives directly benefiting those around us. This is the highest form of resilience. Again, resilience is inherent in each of us because we are made in His image, and we are temples of the Holy Spirit. The degree of submission we operate with in our lives determines the level of resilience we can access. Coincidently, Jesus clearly demonstrated on the earth that living fully is living generously, particularly when it comes to our hearts.

We have discovered the importance of making room in our hearts for others' thoughts and feelings through empathy. As essential as this is, there is one more step in the process of becoming fully resilient leaders; we must move into compassion. In an altruistic fashion, empathy allows us to identify with the emotions and perspectives of another person.

Compassion is the stage where identification moves to action to produce solutions. Compassion is more than an emotion, for it is a compelling force. Think about the occasions where you witnessed something that captured your heart, and in moments, you found yourself responding—you went from feeling to moving, from observation to action. Those moments aren't contingent on your qualifications; instead, they are predicated on your willingness.

I can still remember the way the headlights glimmered on the rain-soaked streets that night when we came upon two young women who had been struck by a car while crossing the street. It was a heart-stopping scene. It felt almost surreal as I saw one woman lying motionless in the middle of the road. Within seconds, I was out of the car and on the ground beside her, face to face.

Immediately I began praying, calling life and healing into her body. Those moments seemed to last forever as I desperately searched for signs of life. Finally, her eyes fluttered open. She began to moan. She was in pain, but she was alive. I stayed with her, encouraging and praying until the ambulance arrived, while the other girl was being attended to by someone else.

By God's grace, she only had a broken leg and minor scrapes. Here is my point—what compelled me into action was not paramedic training but compassion. It moved me out of the comfort of my seat because there was an innocent, injured girl in need. I certainly had no plan, but I didn't need one, because the Spirit of God had the perfect plan.

If you have been in similar situations and have acted, but things didn't work out, the person didn't survive, or you didn't get there in time, don't ever discount the impact your compassionate efforts can make. I have a friend whose father was killed in a motorcycle accident. He died at the scene. An entire year after the accident, at the trial for the woman responsible, a man and woman showed up, saying they had been there when the crash occurred. The woman, a trained nurse, had found my friend's father lying face down in a ditch. He was still breathing. While she cleared the dirt from around his mouth, allowing him to gasp for a few more shallow breaths, she held his hand, she prayed, and he did not die alone. What a comfort the compassionate actions of this nurse were to my friend and her grieving family. While the man didn't make it, that singular act of compassion was not in vain.

We see instances like this continually demonstrated in Jesus' life. "And when Jesus went out He saw a great multitude; and He was moved with compassion for them, and healed their sick" (Matthew 14:14, NKJV). We must learn to condition ourselves to lean into His heart. It will never be convenient to help someone in a time of need, but it will always benefit others and ourselves. You may never know the impact of your actions. Do them anyway. Step forward boldly in compassion.

Perhaps we need to stop hesitating and start responding when He says to move. I don't know about you, but I do not want to stand in front of my Lord at the end of my life and hear about all the moments I failed to respond when and where He was prompting me to action. Sometimes it is simply to speak up on behalf of someone else when you see injustice. Other times it may be to merely purchase a coffee for the person behind you in the drive-through. When we become this expression of love to the world, the world will sit up and take notice, as will heaven.

Resilience is within you. It is life-giving and life-fulfilling. It may appear to be dormant. But remember—Lazarus was in the tomb for four days. Four days! And our sweet, loving, empathetic, compassionate Lord rose him from his slumber. He breathed life into his lungs and introduced him to a second chance at life.

You may feel as though you've been in a tomb for four years; perhaps you're standing at the stone, just waiting to roll it to the side.

RESILIENCE

Remember, whatever it is that put you in that tomb in the first place will become a mantle of empathetic blessings to bestow on others the moment the Lord rolls that stone away. Your darkness may seem overwhelming. Your past may feel suffocating. But your story is just beginning.

If Malala can survive a bullet to her temple and change many lives, how much more can those of us who are called by His name and filled with His Holy Spirit change this world around us for good? the Creator of the Universe resides in you for a reason, His reasons, His plans! You were created for greatness. You were created for good-ness. You were created to meet the challenges of this world head-on, become stronger, and pour into those around you as you overflow with the abundance of a life lived sympathetically, empathetically, and compassionately.

This is your moment. Today is the day to roll your stone away. The world is waiting for you. The Lord has made you strong. He also made you vulnerable and in need of His grace. Lean into it. Claim it as your own. Embrace your strengths and weaknesses, your crowns and your scars, and all the stories you've written, heard, and earned along this winding road we call life. Resilience is yours for the taking, and then its fruits are yours for the giving.

As God loves us so, let us also love one another. Day after day, moment-by-moment, don't miss an opportunity to receive and to give. Wherever you are on your journey, determine right here, right now, to lift your eyes, stand tall, and live with your strong, resilient hands and heart open wide.

epilogue

LOVE OF GOD IS THE CORE OF RESILIENCE

"No, in all these things we are more than conquerors through him who loved us."

—ROMANS 8:37 (NIV)

At the core of resilience is the love of God. Romans 8:37 tells us we are more than conquerors because His demonstrated love is our glorious victory. Resilience is not something we manufacture. We can't work up to it. It is received, inherent; He is our source of victory.

1 John reiterates that if you belong to God, He is living in you and is greater than the one in this world.

Resilience is ultimately contingent on the sturdiness of our foundation. We must be rooted and grounded in His love. That is the substance of resilience. Our faith works are a result of His love. Faith and love work together, as do faith and resilience.

There's a significant difference between looking to God for this type of transformational love and living under a religious ideology that says we are sinners saved by grace instead of recognizing that we are justified by grace. That means that we are inherently equipped to handle adversity. It is our choice to allow that love to be the catalyst that brings change into our lives.

If God is for us, who could ever be against us? When we allow that truth to penetrate our hearts and minds, we can stand through difficulty and return to our original form over and over again. That is resilience. That's what prompts us to press into our purpose and not give up even on the darkest of days. That's where we choose resiliency—not after we've had a pity party, but in the place of trial, when we are at the breaking point, submerged in the riptide that is pulling us down, we can choose a stance of holy stubbornness and remember that our God is for us. He sustains us and brings us back to the surface. His truth makes us buoyant, resilient. We should not be surprised when that love is tested, for it is also in that moment that it is proven. In fact, this is how we become rooted in His love! This world needs to see this type of love in operation, and as His Bride, it is up to us to demonstrate this agape, unbreakable, all-consuming, and powerful form of love.

It's time to get back to truth; it's time to help those who are disenfranchised, misguided, and misinformed so they, too, have the ability and endurance to withstand the fiery trial and not be caught off-guard when adversity comes their way.

This doesn't mean we should, nor encourage others to, walk around with an expectation of doom and gloom. However, when the storms rise, it doesn't catch us off-guard, because we have what we need at the moment.

That is what God's love does for us and can do for others. It resides in the deepest part of our souls, a steady source of strength, discernment, patience, and light. It allows us to stand through difficulty and return to our original form when life beats us down.

His love allows you to press into your purpose, return to the surface, and rise when the world knocks you down.

For, "If God is for us, who can be against us?" (Romans 8:31, ESV).